20

FOUR REFORMS
—A Guide for the Seventies

WILLIAM F. BUCKLEY, JR.

FOUR REFORMS

—A Guide for the Seventies

G. P. Putnam's Sons, New York

nemo me impune lacessit
propter
C. DICKERMAN WILLIAMS
iurisconsultus maximus
amicissimus

Introduction

IT is the purpose of this brief book to suggest a few reforms in welfare, tax, justice, and education.

The reforms in question have stirred in my mind, some of them for many years; others are hand-crafted for this volume. All of them are tempered by exposure to experts and, here and there, by sneak-previews before general audiences. A year ago Mr. Charles Walker, the president of Russell Sage College in Troy, New York, asked me to spend a fortnight as a visiting lecturer on campus. This my schedule would not permit, and I told him that what uncommitted moments I could find in the month he bid for me, I would be devoting to research for this book. He came back with the audacious suggestion that since I had it in mind anyway to write a book called *Four Reforms*, I might give four public lectures at his college, one on each of the four reforms. He proposed to invite an "expert" generally acknowledged as abundantly equipped to disagree with me, for the purpose of analyzing that evening's reform, following which there would be questions from the floor and from a special panel of students.

The experience proved stimulating, though the audience was too large to allow for the kind of kneading an idea gets when presented before, say, a seminar. There was no time to write out the speeches, and it is as well that there wasn't, because it has proved useful to assimilate the objections of the critics into the raw outline, and to transcribe what I hope will prove to be a more resilient whole. I am very grateful to Mr. Walker for his ingenious invitation, and to the students and faculty of Russell Sage for serving as anvil. I might add that the material here, and the formulations, are entirely fresh.

And then I asked several scholars to be good enough to give me extensive memoranda touching on various of my proposed reforms. Concerning welfare I sought out Professor Ernest van den Haag. For justice, Professor Delmar Karlen and C. Dickerman Williams, and for education, Professor Roger Freeman. For taxation, I have probed the views of several scholars, and have leaned heavily on research done by Mr. Alan Reynolds of *National Review*. To these gentlemen I am (as is, a fortiori, the Republic) greatly obliged. The former Miss Agatha Schmidt, on whom I have leaned now for making five books intelligible, has most inconsiderately become Mrs. John Dowd, and a mother; but she suspended her domestic duties for long enough to unscramble my thoughts and my prose. Mr. Robin Wu has given me indispensable help with the research; once again, I am indebted to Mr. Joseph Isola for copyreading the manuscript. It bespeaks my respect for her and for the scholars above that I should have sought them out. Here and there I reiterate a proposal that originated with one of these men but the amalgam being so much my own, I do not assign any of the positions I have arrived at to them. I thank them most sincerely for their generous help.

Inevitably, "reforms" that issue from these auspices will be body-searched for ideological bias. I think there will be less of it discovered than one might expect, though

I do not deny that there is a harnessing force which is antistatist in character. The proposed reforms seek to free up constricting molds and to flush out accretions of government, so as to induce a greater freedom of movement. Such freedom should encourage spontaneity, innovation, and individuation. This is not a book on how to solve the welfare problem, but on how to set the stage for solving it; not a bill of particulars on how large the public sector should be made through taxation, but a suggested order of taxation that would scrape away a generation's rust, and lubricate the social imagination; not a formula for stopping crime, but a way to make the apprehension of the criminal likelier; not a way to teach people what they need to know, but a suggestion or two on how to encourage the development of schools in which people are freer than they now are to find education. I think of my reforms as entirely procedural in character.

"To some people," Michael Oakeshott wrote, in perhaps the most resonantly skeptical passage in modern literature about the capacities of government, " 'government' appears as a vast reservoir of power which inspires them to dream of what use might be made of it. They have favorite projects, of various dimensions, which they sincerely believe are for the benefit of mankind, and to capture this source of power, if necessary to increase it, and to use it for imposing their favorite projects upon their fellows is what they understand as the adventure of governing men. They are, thus, disposed to recognize government as an instrument of passion; the art of politics is to inflame and direct desire. Now," he says, "the disposition to be conservative in respect of politics reflects a quite different view of the activity of governing. The man of this disposition understands it to be the business of a government not to inflame passion and give it new objects to feed upon; but to inject into the activities of already too passionate men an ingredient of moderation; to restrain, to deflate, to pacify, and to reconcile; not to stoke the fires of desire, but to damp them down [because] the conjunction of dreaming and ruling generates tyranny."

The strictures are appropriate here. The problem, as it begins to present itself in twentieth-century democratic politics, is how to cope with stratification. A dozen years ago, distinguishing between "conservatives" and "men of the Right," Whittaker Chambers classified himself as of the latter rather than the former on the grounds that conservatives have an inordinate attachment to existing arrangements, while men of the Right welcome the kind of progress—often ruthlessly achieved—that capitalism midwifes. To be a capitalist and also a "conservative," Chambers mused, is to court reaction by standing in the way of a wheel, a stance necessarily awkward because "the logic of the wheel is to turn." We know that the welfare problem in America is a highly vexed one, and that something ought to be done about it. We know that the crime rate has risen beyond "an acceptable rate," to use the curious cliché which ought to be avoided if only because we ought to avoid the contradiction that that which is not "acceptable" is nevertheless being accepted. Tax policies avoid even that appearance of justice which Aristotle held up as indispensable to a defensible society, and education suffers from impositions upon it of abstract extra-educational ideals. Touching all these questions, George McGovern moved to the limelight in the spring of 1972, and much of his following was there because they sensed that the wheel *has* to turn, that it is mired down and needs now to move. The suggestions of McGovern are not the subject of this essay, except that one notes that in the early days of his second term, before he was distracted by Watergate, Richard Nixon manifestly felt the need to move organically, an exercise no doubt of those political sensibilities that brought on his political primacy. It is not intended as an animadversion on anyone to note that after the primary in Wisconsin in 1972, pollsters discovered that although on the formal political spectrum they occupied antipodal positions, the great majority of those who voted for George Wallace listed as their second choice George McGovern, and many who voted for McGovern listed Wallace as their second choice. Similarly, many young people who had worked for Goldwater in 1964 were, four years later, working for Robert Kennedy. There is a social edginess in the air, and I think it will not be appeased without reforms. The plea here is that these should be primarily procedural rather than substantive. Let the substantive reforms spring up in the terrain made available by the cleared underbrush.

Richard Goodwin has remarked that, most of the time, procedure *is* policy. It is true that procedure can suggest congenial policy. If the filibuster, as procedure, is tolerated, the filibusterer—however negatively—determines policy. If procedures in criminal proceedings extensively increase the rights and the privileges of the defendant class, policy will issue: there will be less punishment and, one supposes, more crime. We have seen that procedures aimed at effecting racial desegregation become basic educational policy.

In this sense, such fresh procedures as I shall outline do incline towards certain policies, and I shall try very hard not to be forgetful, let alone coy, when it is appropriate manfully to suggest what these policies are likely to be. But it should not matter. The First Amendment guaranteeing the freedom of speech (it is nothing more than a procedural guarantee) absolutely guarantees a measure of verbal licentiousness, but that is not the most conspicuous consequence of free speech, let alone a conclusive argument against free speech. If certain reforms in tax policy, or in jurisprudential arrangements, make more likely certain effects than others, the coincidence, even if a causal relation is proven, is not sufficient grounds to invalidate the procedure. Even if it is known with scientific certainty that to raise the speed limit ten miles per hour along a particular highway will increase yearly fatalities along that highway by 10 percent, a faster speed limit is not, on these grounds alone, ruled out.

I attach to this introduction two proposals, or reforms, which I prescind from the others. That decision is arbitrary, and I do not dwell on the reasons for it. It suffices to say only that I wished to deal at lesser length with them. One, so far as I am aware, is altogether original. The other is very old hat, and it is wearisome even to think of rehearsing all the arguments in favor and all the arguments against it, so well known are they. I mean the proposal in favor of a single term for the President of the United States, a term of six years.

In recent months the old-time opponents of the Twenty-second Amendment limiting a President to two terms have spoken out for repealing it, in favor of the status quo ante. They will tell you that the Amendment in question was a morbid bill of attainder against the memory of a dead man whom all the forces of reaction could not beat while he was alive. Let us assume that this is the case, without conceding that because the Amendment was churlishly motivated, it was for that reason unsound. But surely the arguments favor going beyond the Twenty-second Amendment, rather than returning in the other direction. The principal argument for a one-term executive, it seems to me—and note once again that we are dealing with a procedural rather than a substantive reform—is that the power of the Executive, however much everyone from left to right seeks to control it in the years and decades to come, will remain inordinate unless such organic revisions of the Constitution are undertaken as, in point of fact, never will be. It is not only instructive but amusing to sit about, as the scholars do at Santa Barbara, composing models for a very different republic. Perhaps if the Founding Fathers had been separated by more than just a few years from the opprobrious memory of George III they would have shown less hostility to the idea of a monarch who, whatever his powers two hundred years ago when kings were sure-enough kings and queens queens, would by now have been thoroughly domesticated, even as in England, and left to perform functions primarily ceremonial. But even these functions are very important, and august, and enhance enormously the prestige and therefore the subtle power of the American President who performs them. Presidents are very much conscious of their singularity as, simultaneously, chief of government and chief of state. When President Eisenhower went to the summit in Geneva in 1955 to meet with Eden, Bulganin, and Fauvre, he declined, when the projected schedule was elaborated before him, to act even as primus inter pares. The co-celebrants were tactfully reminded that there existed back home a flesh-and-blood Queen of England, a President of Russia, and a President of France, no one of whom was present at Geneva; whereas the American was both executive *and* titular representative of his country, and should be treated with appropriate diplomatic deference.

These, as I say, are bygones, and it is simply idle to talk about reforms in the Constitution of a kind that would divide the power of the Presidency among more people. But there *is* sentiment for the moderate suggestion to limit the President to a single term; and not inconceivably, perhaps after a President during his second term leaves a particularly sour taste (the incumbent, who endorses the reform, might serve the purpose well), a Presidential candidate will include in his platform a promise to back an amendment that would limit his term to six years.

Grant the hypothetical disadvantage—that destiny might at some great historical juncture vouchsafe us a Periclean figure whose continued service we would not want to deprive ourselves of. But even as matters now stand, we could have Pericles only for two more years beyond the projected six. The opposite argument, that we would need to wait six long years before getting rid of a bad President, is best reduced to size by reminding ourselves that we would need to wait only two years more than we now have to wait; and anyway, the only two Presidents in this century who were defeated after their first term (Taft and Hoover) could each have served another two years with minimum distress to the Republic, and possibly with great advantage to it.

The House of Representatives is continuously there to transcribe the popular will (and oblige it on those few occasions when it is truly hortatory), and Congress can take action affirmative or negative—including action to vitiate or ignore Presidential initiatives. But there is the institutional argument for encouraging the more strategic uses of the Presidency, and I find it hard to understand why the procedure is not slightly modified so as to encourage Presidents to take the longer view they cannot safely take when a reelection contest lies implacably before them.

And then there is the question of the aged.

Mr. James Michener says it bluntly, that in his opinion the problem of caring for the aged looms as the principal social problem of the balance of this century: greater than ecological asphyxiation, greater than overpopulation, greater than the energy crisis. The figure is, I suppose, scientific impressionism, but it has been said that one-half of those who are now sixty-five years or older would be dead if medical science had been arrested even a generation ago. It is absolutely predictable that medical progress will continue, and with it the successes of gerontology.

Already it is a subject one shrinks from dwelling upon—the years and years between the time when men and women are, if the word can be used in this context, ripe to die, and the day that increasing millions will die. Euthanasia, pending word to the contrary from the Supreme Court, is unthinkable. The cost of caring for the aged, most of whom need supervisory medical attention on a continuing basis, is suggested by this recent datum, namely, that the daily cost of a semiprivate hospital room in New York City is now over one hundred dollars. Good private homes for the aged are beyond the reach of any except the very very few. There are charitable and religious homes that will take in elderly people in return for their Social Security checks. But these—I think, for example, of the Mary Manning Walsh home in New York City—are necessarily exclusive, with facilities cruelly unequal to the task at hand.

The physical facilities and professional services needed for the aged are extremely expensive, and there is no way to avoid the capital cost of them. Certainly there is no reason to discourage the private sector from addressing itself as vigorously as possible to the building of suitable homes. Professional medical aid will have to be furnished by doctors and highly trained nurses, the cost of whose services is high, and will probably get higher.

The only variable is in the cost of unskilled labor. And the only human leaven is youth, whose functional companionship could greatly affect the quality of the last years.

The Mary Manning Walsh home in New York employs full time 40 doctors and 43 registered nurses. The cadre of its professional staff is 50. It employs, as

cooks, waiters, janitors, nurses' assistants, elevator opera-
tors, laboratory workers, a total of 311. There are 347
beds in the home, so that the ratio of unskilled employees
per patient is very nearly one for one. Or, taking the
figures for the nation, in 1969 there were 850,000
Americans in nursing homes that employed 444,000
people, or one employee for 1.9 patients. (In 1963, there
were 491,000 resident patients of nursing homes, so that
in six years the figures almost doubled.)

The Republic faces a crisis of a very particular and
very poignant kind. We are aware of the reasons why less
and less the aged die at home. The principal reason is the
lengthening life span. Another is the need for certain
kinds of care that cannot readily be provided at home.
Another is the diminishing domestic utility of the great-
grandmother or great-grandfather. Still another is the
very high cost of urban living quarters where, now, 73
percent of the American people live. All of these combine
to create the institution of the nursing home.

Simultaneous with the increase in the aged is the
increase in the college population. That population in
1930 was 1.1 million. In 1970, 8.4 million.

It is my proposal that the burden of the nonprofes-
sional work done in behalf of the aged should be done by
young men and women graduated from high school,
during one year before matriculating at college. The idea
of public service of some kind or another by the citizenry
has frequently been proposed. There has been an instinc-
tive coolness towards the idea primarily because of the
conscriptive feel of it: the suggestion that government
require anyone to do anything of a philanthropic character tends to put one off, and for reasons not by any means
all bad. The opportunity is great for initiative from the
private sector.

I envision a statement by the trustees of the ten
top-rated private colleges and universities in the United

States in which it is given as common policy that beginning in the fall semester of 1976 (to pick a year far enough away to permit planning, soon enough to generate excitement), no one accepted into the freshman class will be matriculated until after he has passed one year in public service. I say public service because if the plan were very widely adopted, there would be more young help available than could be absorbed in the nursing homes alone. There are many other ways in which the young could be used. As guards in the grade schools, just to give a single example (there are 1,700 auxiliaries in the New York schools alone), but for convenience I dwell on the care of the aged.

As regards the financing, it would be required only that the government exclude this category of volunteers from the provisions of the minimum wage. Otherwise the economic advantage would substantially dissipate. The nursing homes would of course provide board and pocket money (mostly, the volunteers could continue to live at home). In the unusual case where the eighteen-year-old is helping to support his own family, the college could either suspend the requirement or concert with foundations to find ways to permit the young volunteers to eke out the year.

The colleges would take the position that they desire, in matriculating freshmen, an earnest of public concern, and extra-academic experience of a useful kind. The intervention of hundreds of thousands of eighteen-year-olds into the lives of the aged would serve more than merely the obvious purposes of cleaning the rooms and pushing the wheelchairs and washing the dishes. It would mean, for the aged, continuing contact with young, spirited people in their most effusive years. For the young it would mean several things. It would postpone by a year their matriculation at college. College administrators are all but unanimous in their conviction that an older student, one year, rather than freshly graduated, from high school gets more out of college. The experience would, moreover, interrupt the inertial commitment to more-and-more education, and some of the less strongly motivated, the rhythm having been broken, would probably elect not to go on to college. The experience—particularly because of the voluntary aspect of it—would remind young people at an impressionable age of the nature of genuine, humanitarian service, which is the disinterested personal act of kindness, administered by one individual directly to another individual. And the experience would touch the young, temperamentally impatient with any thought of the other end of the life cycle, with the reality of old age; with the human side of the detritus whose ecological counterparts have almost exclusively occupied fashionable attention in recent years. Their capacity to give pleasure to others, without the stimulant of sex, or the pressure of the peer group, or the sense of family obligation, or the lure of economic reward, could not help but reinforce the best instincts of American youth, and these instincts are unstimulated at our peril. What it might provide for society as a whole, this union of young and old, is, just possibly, the reestablishment of a lost circuit: of spirit, and affection, and understanding.

WM. F. BUCKLEY, JR.

Stamford, Connecticut, October 1, 1973

CHAPTER I

Welfare

Towards a Sensible Welfare System

IT is gnawingly clear that welfare arrangements in America aren't working. When Mr. Lindsay ran for mayor of New York City in 1965, he promised that welfare would be reduced, economies instituted, and the indigent revived. As it worked out, welfare tripled during Mr. Lindsay's tenure. Nor can we leave the problem with the happy assumption that New York City is uniquely victimized in virtue of the concentration there of municipal mismanagement, structural sloth, ideological rodomontade, and economic profiteering. In fact, New York City does not stand out, at one welfare case per seven inhabitants, as the worst in the country, if by worst we mean the city with the highest percentage of welfare recipients. Baltimore, St. Louis, and San Francisco are as bad, and Boston (one in five) considerably worse. The trouble is widespread, and recognized by leaders of every political division. As far away as 1967, Senator Robert Kennedy was saying that the welfare system ought to be thrown out, though he did not elaborate an alternative. Except for the guaranteed annual wage, nobody really has; and, of course, the guaranteed annual wage, or the negative income tax, is less a reform than a capitulation.

The objectives of the myriad federal and state welfare measures have always been plain. The idea is first of all to help people, people who in the absence of concrete help will suffer deprivations the community does not suffer them to suffer. The idea is, in effect, to capitalize these people during the implicitly brief period of transition until the wealth-oriented dynamic of American society picks them up, dusts them off, and sets them down on the road to self-sustenance and relative affluence, at once relieving the community of the particular burden, enhancing the well-being of the community by the contributions of the rehabilitated, and relieving human beings of the spiritual ignominy of dependence.

Much thought has been given, particularly in recent months and years, to the philosophy of welfarism. On some points most people are agreed. But on fewer points than, say, a decade ago. There are reasons for this, practical and philosophical. We are an empirical society, achievement-oriented. Our failure to eliminate poverty through welfarism has caused not only many politicians to wonder, but some social philosophers to question the further dogmas of welfarism, more or less a posteriori. It is questionable that anyone would object to welfarism in almost any form if one's historical experience with it had been that in fact it had progressively reduced, to the point of eliminating, poverty.

Among the points worth weighing, even in anticipation of a reform that is strictly procedural in nature, are the following.

1. Enthusiasts for the marketplace are for the most part prepared not so much to "concede"—that is not the right word, because morally serious free-market philosophers have never maintained that the market judgment is the moral judgment, John Bates Clark notwithstanding nor,

ad astra per aspera, Ayn Rand—as to *proceed on the assumption* that the market does not by any means necessarily reward the best, the brightest, and the most benevolent. They insist only—we insist—that a judgment made against the market is itself arbitrary, and functionally dislocative. *I* know that an evening with Pablo Casals playing J. S. Bach is more rewarding than an evening with the Rolling Stones playing J. S. Evanescent, but I simply cannot unwinkingly construct a defensible society that requires that Casals earn more than Mick Jagger, or that Florence Nightingale should earn more than Diamond Jim Brady. The best I can do is promise to be utterly undazzled by the man who corners the soybean market, and utterly humbled by Quiller-Couch, but I must keep my sticky fingers out of the marketplace.

Of course, acquiescence in the general proposition that one must not reorder the marketplace so as to make its rewards correspond with our idea of what should be rewarded, is not to take a vow of noninterference of any kind. Some interference in behalf of some kinds of welfare is generally accepted, and the proper basis for levying for such redistribution will be discussed in the ensuing chapter. It remains only to be said that categorical opposition to welfare of any kind is not a part of the philosophical equipment of the libertarians of this world whose objections, we note tirelessly once again, tend to be procedural, with all the gravity that that word can command.

2. Poverty, after a certain point, is a subjective rather than an objective condition. A recent and genuinely pathetic portrait of the life of an employee of a major automobile company in Detroit brings the point home. It is observed that the father and mother and four children permit themselves to dine away from the home kitchen only once a month, and then only at a hamburger

restaurant on the day that they see the monthly outdoor movie, the only one they patronize because that weekday it permits the entire cargo of an automobile in at the blanket price of $2.50. The wife washes, dries, and irons all the family's clothes, except the blue jeans and the husband's shirts. The husband takes care of everything in the house that requires maintenance, but last fall he had to order a new furnace, which he bought on time and will be paying the bank for over the next four years, alongside the payments he makes for his car, which he trades in every four years. The boy goes for two weeks during the summer to a camp administered by their church. At that, the drain of $75 is a grave lesion on the exchequer. The girls go once a week to the nearest beach and take along a picnic lunch to avoid the higher cost, along the boardwalk, of frankfurters and orange pop. They have Blue Cross, and the father has not missed a day of work in ten years, but his savings are only $700. At home they have the usual accessories, including an air-conditioning unit in the living room. Travel is out of the question, except for the Christmas trip in the car when they alternate between the two sets of grandparents. They live for the day when the last of the children has finished school, and retirement pay begins. By the time they have reached Social Security, they reason, the restriction against earning extra money will be withdrawn. They now earn just under $10,000 per year.

If such a family is to be pitied in America, it is nevertheless to be envied in most of the rest of the world. By current standards 50 percent of the American people were poor as recently as in 1920. But the pain, to judge from one's knowledge of the literature of protest of the twenties, is more acute today than then. The statistics are almost uniformly reassuring, and have been for many years. Between 1935 and 1950 the income earned by the top quintile of Americans advanced by 32 percent, while the bottom quintile went up by 125 percent, or at a rate four times as great. Between 1956 and 1967 median white income rose 46 percent. Median black income rose by 76 percent. By 1970 the startling figure was in—there remained a virtually insignificant difference in the income of young (under thirty-five) white and black couples.

But in any society in which there are significant differences in income, which is to say in every society with the debatable exception of Maoist society, there will be an upper quintile which will be called rich and a lower quintile which will be called poor. Moreover, as indicated, it does not follow that the higher the level of income of the lowest quintile, the less the dissatisfaction, but very nearly the opposite. The higher it moves, the more acute the dissatisfaction. "While the inevitable is tolerated," Mr. van den Haag has written, "the inadequate is always resented."

3. Beyond the vague injunction to care for one's brother, there is no welfare ethic crystallized to the point of indicating exactly what are the obligations of the rich to the poor; or, more accurately, of the nonpoor to the poor. As a rule of thumb, the conservative has stressed the ideal of freedom, while the (American) liberal has stressed the ideal of equality. Professor Amnon Rubinstein, himself a socialist, made a grudging, though elegant, admission in a television colloquy a year or two ago in Israel: "On the whole," he said, "those systems that have put liberty ahead of equality have done better by equality than those that have put equality above liberty." Mr. Rubinstein was touching lightly on the disputed question, concerning which there is no intention here to be disputatious, that it has proved, on the whole, easier to lift the income of the whole of a people—as one

would lift a mobile, each member occupying, at the new elevation, the same distance it occupied before from the members just above him, and way above him—than to lift the income of only the lowest members of the mobile. The American experience, as the figures show, is very good not only at lifting the whole mobile, but, in the process, at reducing the number that continue to hang below the poverty level—from 50 percent to 9 percent in fifty years is pretty dazzling. But all of this does not settle the questions: what is it that we are doing wrong; what is it that we should be doing more of; what is it that we should be doing less of; and what is it that we propose to do if it should prove that the graph away from poverty is asymptotic, that we are coming now up against an entrenched minority—the structurally poor, to use the term fashionable during the sixties; and what distinctions should we observe, and how observe them, between self-inflicted poverty (the mother who continues to have illegitimate children, the alcoholic, the drug addict) and innocent poverty (the blind, the dependent children)?

4. We begin to have a few insights on the bureaucracy of welfare. One notes that, for welfare, there is an elastic clientele—which is not to say that the opposite is true, namely that to diminish welfare is to diminish, *pro tanto*, welfare eligibles.

But focus first on the positive formulation. Increase the dollars pumped into the welfare system, and you will increase the number of people who crop up to claim them, or the amounts claimed by existing clients—generally both. Even though during the sixties unemployment declined and real income increased at all levels, the welfare rolls grew. And there was no prospect in sight for their diminution until (as we shall see) there was direct intervention. If the Congress had voted, say, another $10 billion for welfare programs of various kinds—in education, in child care, in medical care, in free food—it is no longer seriously doubted that the response would have been totally elastic, i.e., that the increase in availability would have met with a corresponding increase in takers.

On the other hand, eliminating welfare to Point Zero would not result in eliminating welfare clients to Zero— the blind and the lame, the mothers with little babies present and demanding food and shelter, will not disappear. The question of how far in the direction of Zero, or how far in the other direction, state-administered welfare should go is a question of fine moral, political, and economic tuning. To go too far in one direction is to encourage a parasitic class. To go too far in the other direction is to approach misanthropy. Where to stop along the scale requires adjudication of value-hierarchies that differ, as reasonable men might differ on the extent of the obligation of one economic class to another; and of differences between experts who represent either directly conflicting claims about what happens when you give X amount, or different judgments on the efficacy of stopping at this point or the other in the scale, the one insisting that less welfare is strategically more benevolent, the other that more welfare is more benevolent, that tactical satisfaction is what counts, not strategic smugness: and so on.

The rise in the welfare rolls was from 7 million in 1962 to 16 million in 1972. Americans, as we have noted, crossed the poverty line in their deliberate way, giving great statistical satisfaction. Adjusting for the value of the dollar (which, by the way, I shall do throughout this essay when it makes sense to do so, without again bringing the matter up), the 50 percent poor in 1920, by the standards of the Johnson Administration, reduced to 20 percent in 1960, to 11 percent in 1967, and is said nowadays to be in the vicinity of 9 percent or even less. Even so, during the past decade of intensive welfare activity, welfare rolls grew and grew and grew. It is deduced from the gross figures that what happened to make the poverty rolls grow was less the multiplication of poor people than the wide advertisement of the availability of welfare subsidies. Mr. Irving Kristol has written that he can easily understand taxpayers' resenting certain welfare programs, but that he cannot understand taxpayers' resenting it when people reach out for welfare benefits whose availability is pointed out to them. Professor Nathan Glazer has observed that, ten years ago, 10 percent of the Negroes in New York City were receiving welfare, but that in 1971 the figure was 35 percent, notwithstanding that real and relative black income greatly increased during that decade.

Grief over the failure of welfarism is shared now by those who resent the cost of the programs, those who care less about the cost than about the grating inutility of the programs, and those theorists of welfarism who are demoralized, or discredited.

And so, under the pressure of public protest, state and city politicians have begun to look at the welfare system. They have very little choice. Quite apart from any academic or even political concern, there was the lowering economic problem. If the graph continued to rise at the same angle over the next ten years as over the past ten, the state would simply have no money left over, say, in California or New York, for anything else—for cutting the grass in the parks, or providing pensions for legislators. From 1960 to 1970, the annual cost of California's welfare program had quadrupled to more than $2.5 billion. The welfare rolls had grown from 600,000 to 2.2 million and were continuing to grow by 40,000 each month. Moreover, since in 1970 the federal government was paying 43 percent of California's welfare bill, and since California was contributing to the federal government about as much as the federal government was returning to California, the projected increase in California's welfare burden, consulting all the taxpayers' ledgers, was intolerable. Something had to be done about it, and individual state leaders took the initiative.

Not only in California. Mr. Nelson Rockefeller, having at one point rejected the recommendations of a commission of his own appointees that the state legislature discourage impulsive immigration into New York, now suddenly reversed himself and instituted a residency requirement. There was much discussion about what effect, if any, a residency requirement (one year before you can line up for a welfare check) might have on such an immigrants' cynosure as New York State. New York State would not find out. The Supreme Court ruled (apropos of Connecticut) in 1969 (*Shapiro v. Thompson*) that by prescribing residency requirements New York State's legislature was, in effect, trying to regulate traffic, and that inasmuch as that prerogative had been specifically reserved by the Constitution to Congress, state laws requiring residency requirements for recipients of monies that had in part been appropriated by Congress were constitutionally presumptuous, hence void.

A year or so later, New York officials began to enforce a law, largely ignored over the years since it had been passed, to the effect that able-bodied and mobile welfare applicants can be summoned to duty. Over a period of about one year, from 1971 to 1972, 25,000 New Yorkers did, in fact, present themselves for training and work—and many of them, it is maintained by municipal officials, performed usefully, and some began to learn a trade. That law was then shot down by the district court. The court held that a state cannot impose conditions on the distribution of federal money if those conditions are not imposed by the Congress. The Supreme Court has since (June, 1973) overruled the district court, but it is too early to judge the results of the restoration of that reform, or to know exactly what is the settled legal situation.

In the area we are here primarily concerned with—aid to the poor—the ground rules are set by the individual states. Federal money is remitted in the form of subsidies to the states for use in the various social insurance measures. The federal subsidies, designed to help the poorer states, compose a larger percentage of the welfare money handed out in, say, Mississippi (83 percent) than New York (44 percent). In theory, if a state rejected the federal supplement, it could proceed, unmolested, to prescribe its own qualifications for recipients, provided it did not discriminate among them unconstitutionally. In theory, a state could abolish most forms of social insurance (the obvious exception is Social Security); as a practical matter, for reasons the implications of which are about to be examined, this is not feasible.

In California, Mr. Ronald Reagan has undertaken a number of inquiries and reforms. Conspicuous among them are three: (1) He has insisted that fathers who abandon their children, whether legitimate or illegitimate, should be tracked down and held accountable for the support of their families. It is no part of any civil liberty written or unwritten, Mr. Reagan reasons, for a live and productive father to bequeath, ad libitum, his wife, civil or common-law, and children, legitimate or natural, to the state. (2) He has attempted to institutionalize an important distinction. Even though we recognize that the line between, at one end, a man irremediably blind and, at the other, a man temporarily disabled by whooping cough, is not easily divided so as to distinguish the category of the permanently disabled from the category of the temporarily disabled, nevertheless it is better to segregate the obvious extremes, with the view to helping the one permanently, the other temporarily. Accordingly, Mr. Reagan has sought to establish plausible frontiers. The objective is to treat the one category as though it were receiving Social Security checks—forever, no questions asked. And (3) to devise imaginative means of treating those in the other category once they become employable again. They are, in effect, temporary employees of the state. The idea is to pay such persons at the end of every week during which they have performed assigned duties, or submitted to training programs. Early returns are encouraging. (An interesting dividend: rather than submit to work or training, many Californians previously on welfare—the figures are incomplete—elected to withdraw their claims.) After two years California had 274,000 fewer welfare cases, saving $1 billion over the welfare cost had it continued rising at the 1965–1971 rate.

No state that I know of has yet attempted to etch out a distinction considered crucial by Mr. Roger Starr of New York, the gifted writer and student of city welfare problems. He believes that the relevant distinction is growing not so much as between the permanently and temporarily disabled, as between the "disorganized" poor and the transient poor. In New York City, he writes, there are many adults (he guesses at the figure of 100,000) who are so thoroughly "disorganized" that they do not respond to any of the stimuli that have prompted people in the past to will their way out of poverty. Mr. Starr is talking about families that do not qualify even to live in public housing. There are far fewer public housing units than applicants for them. Accordingly, officials who administer them consult not only economic, but noneconomic factors. They inquire into the habits of the family making the application. If the father is alcoholic and the mother doesn't send her children off to school, if the kids exercise themselves by knocking old men or old ladies off the sidewalks, they are excluded. What then? Where do they go to live? How does the state go about invigorating an ethos so greatly etiolated? It is his insight that any failure to accost the special problems of the disorganized poor is a failure to accost what may well prove to be the major problem of a society concerned about welfare. But all programs designed to deal with basic human motivation are of course experimental. And experimentation is made difficult by existing arrangements.

It is so in the matter of incentive. Although it is all but impossible to find anyone who defends the idea that welfare payments should be reduced dollar-for-dollar against income earned, that continues to be the infuriating practice. One or two critics of the welfare system, notably Ernest van den Haag, have argued that we experiment with exactly the opposite policy: that instead of reducing welfare for those who begin to earn money in the market, we increase it. In other words, that we reinforce the incentive to work by putting a premium on it—up to a point, needless to say. (A logical extension of that insight, surely, is to effect a minimum wage not by impositions on employers, but by subsidies to employees.) As things now stand, in New York City the head of a family of four can take $318 a month in welfare untaxed (not counting Medicaid and food stamps), or if he works forty hours at the minimum wage, he can earn $286 of taxable salary.

One notes, briefly, that thought, some of it orderly, most of it desultory, is being given to what is everywhere recognized as a problem. Some reforms are being attempted, but the scope and shape of them are greatly affected by budgets heavily controlled by Washington. Some attempted reforms or experiments are shot down by the courts. Still others are advanced tentatively, as imprudent for experimentation on a national scale. We are without the mobility to move productively, energetically, enthusiastically, and this is so because great superstitions have enthralled the Republic, and ignorance has dimmed our vision. The required reform is procedural in nature, yet it is as liberating in its implications as the procedural guarantee of habeas corpus.

❦

A proposed reform:
Congress shall appropriate funds for social welfare only for the benefit of those states whose per capita income is below the national average.

❦

Why does Congress concern itself with the welfare problem of states whose resources, per capita, are above those of the average state?

With the exception of Social Security and Medicare (programs that engage the federal government directly with the individual), welfare programs of the categorical kind are handled through the states. The purpose of these programs is redistributionist—i.e., to take from those who have more than they need in order to give to those who have less than they need, or in any case less than the government thinks they ought to have. The state's own resources, under the circumstances, is a critical datum. You do not construct relief programs for the benefit of a Rockefeller. By the same token, you should not construct relief programs for the benefit of New York State. It is not a part of the stated rationale of American welfare programs to give money to states perfectly capable of executing their own redistributionist programs.

Yet that, as we all know, is precisely what is being done. Not everybody knows the extent of the ongoing incoherence. To know that, one needs to experience the figures. These figures, for all that they speak resoundingly about the central paradoxes of redistributionism within a federal system, are strangely unknown. And nowhere, that I have seen, are they even superficially analyzed.

What follows on pages 34–37 is a list of the states of the Union (I include the District of Columbia because the official charts do) followed by columns of figures.

Running one's eyes over the figures, one is hit by the anomalies. They recur, but I mention only the first in each category, beginning at the top with New York State.

Taking the first state, we learn

—New York ranks as the leading per capita earner in the Union.

—the earnings of New Yorkers average around $5,000 per person.

—for every dollar turned over by the federal government to the state of New York for welfare purposes, 98 cents is taken by the federal government in taxes from the state of New York.

—New York paid in taxes to the federal government 10.9 percent of the entire sum taxed by the federal government.

—New York received 11.16 percent of the sum distributed by the federal government as "revenue sharing."

—New York paid 98 cents (the figure is coincidentally the same as above), out to the federal government for every dollar it took in under revenue sharing.

What, pray, is the wealthiest state in the Union doing as a net beneficiary of federal tax dollars? Not by very much—a mere 2 percent—but the figures are adamant.

New York pays in 98 cents, and receives 100 cents in return. This means that every state whose figure in the second column extends to the left of the decimal point is subsidizing New York State. Running down the column until one reaches the poorest of the states that hand out more dollars than they receive, we see, mirabile dictu, Texas—whose per capita income, at $3,726 per person, is $1,274 below New York's, but which is nevertheless sending tax dollars for the relief of New Yorkers.

What is the explanation for New York's anomalous appearance as a state first in per capita wealth, yet patronized by a state which is thirty-first in per capita wealth? The obvious answer is that New York is a more powerful state than Texas. But Texas is hardly helpless— the story is more complicated. Some years ago Congress was so incautious as to enact an open-ended program committing the federal government to matching state and local contributions to a broad line of social programs. Incredibly, the small type in this seizure of Congressional munificence was not discovered right away. But then, in 1970 and 1971, sharp California eyes discovered the bonanza (note the comparable advantages of California, the ninth ranking state, which nevertheless receives a dollar for every 95 cents taxed).

New York was able to qualify all kinds of projects under the required social services designation and so receive hundreds of millions of federal dollars. This became an insiders' cause célèbre, and a $2.5 billion limitation has been proposed on the social services program as an amendment to the general revenue sharing bill. Call it a state-tax loophole. No doubt it can be ironed out, but until the political power of New York and California evaporates, the likelihood is that they will devise other means of lightening, and as in recent years eliminating, their net tax load. They are the state

THE COSTS AND DISTRIBUTION OF FEDERAL AID

(The states are listed in order of decreasing per capita income)

	The state's ranking, by per capita income	Per capita income of the state[1]	The tax burden of the state, per dollar of grants from the federal government[2]	The state's contribution to federal taxes, as a percentage[3]	The state's share of Revenue Sharing expressed as a percentage[4]	The tax burden of the state, per dollar of Revenue Sharing received[5]
D.C.		$5,870	$ .23	.50%	.45%	$1.11
N.Y.	1	5,000	.98	10.90	11.16	.98
Conn.	2	4,995	1.54	2.02	1.25	1.62
Alaska	3	4,875	.33	.17	.12	1.42
Nev.	4	4,822	1.14	.31	.21	1.48
N.J.	5	4,811	1.53	4.38	3.09	1.42
Ill.	6	4,775	1.53	6.49	5.18	1.25
Haw.	7	4,738	.92	.43	.45	.96
Del.	8	4,673	1.49	.35	.30	1.17
Calif.	9	4,640	.95	11.06	10.49	1.05
Mass.	10	4,562	1.12	3.17	3.08	1.03
Md.	11	4,522	1.38	2.19	2.02	1.08
Mich.	12	4,430	1.29	4.60	4.19	1.10
Kans.	13	4,192	1.08	1.02	1.00	1.02
Ohio	14	4,175	1.55	5.33	3.91	1.36

(The average per capita income, U.S. population, $4,156)

Colo.	15	4,153	.81	1.07	1.03	1.04
Penn.	16	4,147	1.22	5.90	5.17	1.14
Wash.	17	4,132	1.02	1.63	1.59	1.03
R.I.	18	4,126	.99	.47	.45	1.04
Minn.	19	4,032	.95	1.72	1.96	.88
Neb.	20	4,030	1.19	.67	.81	.83
Ind.	21	4,027	1.61	2.40	1.97	1.22
Ore.	22	3,959	.85	.98	1.06	.92
Mo.	23	3,940	1.04	2.15	1.86	1.16
Fla.	24	3,930	1.43	3.34	2.75	1.21
Wyo.	25	3,929	.65	.16	.18	.89
Ariz.	26	3,913	.93	.84	.98	.88
Wisc.	27	3,912	1.38	2.01	2.53	.79
Va.	28	3,899	1.04	2.13	1.98	1.08

(The average per capita income of the states, $3,894)

Iowa	29	3,877	1.17	1.20	1.45	.83
N.H.	30	3,796	1.06	.36	.29	1.24
Tex.	31	3,726	1.03	4.93	4.61	1.07

(The principal division between the states that, net, give and those that, net, receive)

Vt.	32	3,638	.57	.19	.28	.68
Mont.	33	3,629	.53	.29	.39	.74

THE COSTS AND DISTRIBUTION OF FEDERAL AID (*Continued*)
(The states are listed in order of decreasing per capita income)

	The state's ranking, by per capita income	Per capita income of the state[1]	The tax burden of the state, per dollar of grants from the federal government[2]	The state's contribution to federal taxes, as a percentage[3]	The state's share of Revenue Sharing expressed as a percentage[4]	The tax burden of the state, per dollar of Revenue Sharing received[5]
Geo.	34	$3,599	$.76	1.86%	2.07%	$.90
N. Dak.	35	3,538	.54	.23	.37	.62
Okla.	36	3,515	.65	1.02	1.12	.91
Utah	37	3,442	.63	.41	.59	.69
S. Dak.	38	3,441	.57	.23	.47	.49
N. Car.	39	3,424	.85	1.93	2.56	.75
Idaho	40	3,409	.75	.27	.38	.71
Maine	41	3,375	.69	.38	.59	.64
Ky.	42	3,306	.61	1.17	1.65	.71
Tenn.	43	3,300	.70	1.51	1.86	.81
N. Mex.	44	3,298	.43	.38	.63	.60
W. Va.	45	3,275	.46	.66	.99	.67
La.	46	3,252	.60	1.31	2.14	.61

S. Car.	47	3,142	.68	.88	1.54	.57
Ala.	48	3,087	.51	1.14	2.19	.52
Ark.	49	3,078	.54	.63	1.04	.61
Miss.	50	2,788	.33	.63	1.71	.37

[1] Tax Foundation, *Facts and Figures on Government Finance: 1973*. Data are for calendar year 1971.

[2] Tax Foundation, "Memorandum on Allocation of The Federal Tax Burden and Federal Grants-In-Aid By State" (February 15, 1972). Excludes Revenue Sharing; includes highway aids, unemployment compensation and employment service administration aids, and airport and airway grants-in-aid. Fiscal 1971.

[3] Tax Foundation, "Memorandum on Allocation of The Federal Tax Burden" (January 17, 1973). For fiscal year 1973.

[4] *U.S. News & World Report*, October 9, 1972. Calculated from the allocation of 1972 general "Revenue Sharing" payments ($5.3 billion) by state.

[5] Estimated by dividing the percent of federal taxes paid, by state, by the percent of Revenue Sharing received (Notes 3 & 4 above). This is necessarily an approximation because the latest available Revenue Sharing data are for a calendar year, while the tax burden data are for a fiscal year. The tax burden by state is, however, fairly constant from year to year, so that different time periods have an insignificant effect on the final column.

equivalent of the man with the million dollars of income who pays no taxes.

Connecticut is the second ranking state in the Union, and Connecticut is altogether philanthropic in its relations with Washington, no doubt in part because Connecticut is a very little state. Although its per capita income is only $5 less than New York's, it pays out not 98 cents for every federal dollar it receives, but $1.54. At that, Connecticut's net disadvantage is not the greatest in the Union. Ohio is the fourteenth ranking state, but turns in an extra penny over Connecticut's for each dollar returned—$1.55. And Indiana, as the twenty-first state, turns in the highest figure—$1.61. Indiana and Ohio, in other words, are the prime statistical victims in the game of federal redistribution.

The third ranking state, Alaska, is wildly offbeat, turning in 33 cents and receiving $1. The anomaly, however, is safely disregarded, on the grounds that the vastness of Alaska and the sparseness of the population combine to polarize the figures. Alaska is more interesting as regards its share of revenue sharing. Revenue sharing is a means of getting money back to the states as a supplement over and above the grants-in-aid. The measure, as the figures immediately reveal, was wildly political and jury-rigged. In the case of Alaska one sees that the Alaskan lobby was all but powerless to maintain the profitable ratio of the grants-in-aid. Thus Alaska, paying .17 percent of federal taxes, received as its share of Revenue Sharing only .12 percent, for a ratio of 1.42.

Next in line is Nevada. Though the fourth ranking state, it is rather narrowly a patron, at $1.14 sent to Washington in return for the dollar received.

New Jersey and Illinois are more or less properly situated according to their means.

Hawaii, though the seventh wealthiest, is remote and

largely undeveloped, and so shares the same welfare advantages, though not so pronouncedly, as Alaska. Note that in Revenue Sharing, Hawaii is not, like Alaska, penalized. This could be a special recognition of Hawaii's problems, or just plain Oversight.

Colorado, the fifteenth wealthiest state, is, at 81 cents to Washington for one dollar back, a substantial beneficiary considering its advantaged position as fifteenth ranking state.

What is most interesting about Wisconsin is the discrepancy between its two net positions. Though down to twenty-seventh in rank, it pays $1.38 for every federal dollar. But Revenue Sharing, perhaps from bad conscience, drastically altered the ratio to 79 cents taxed for every dollar returned. The sum total of Revenue Sharing funds, however, was $5.3 billion, compared to the grants-in-aid total of $29.09 billion, so that compensatory efforts via revenue sharing are mere palliatives.

The average state per capita income falls between the twenty-eighth and twenty-ninth states—between Virginia and Iowa. The figure is $3,894.*

The three states that fall immediately below this average figure are Iowa, New Hampshire, and Texas. They are nevertheless, though just slightly, in the philanthropic category, giving more than they receive.

The sharp fall-off into the category of the beneficiary states begins abruptly with the thirty-second state, right after Texas. Vermont, though its income is only $88 per capita less than Texas', is greatly favored by the tax ratio. As one descends the ladder passing seventeen states to Mississippi, the poorest state of the Union with $2,788 per capita income, there are discrepancies; even so, on

---

* The per capita average income calculated without any reference to the states is much higher—$4,156. What this means is very simply that the higher income states tend to be more highly populated than the poorer states.

the whole, these nineteen states are clearly beneficiaries of the welfare tax system.

But notice this. The nineteen lowest states paid in a total of $5,098.0 million for $8,212.8 million in grants and revenue sharing. For every dollar they paid to the government, they took back $1.61. On the strength of all of which we note that the net movement of money towards the nineteen poorest states ($3,114.8 million) is a mere 9 percent of the entire sum of money involved.

The population of the 19 states is 41,634,000. The net subsidy, in per capita figures, amounts to $74.81.

A few objections come to mind.

1. It is deceptive (it will be argued) to accept the per capita income figures as though they exactly reflected true differences in the economic standing of the states. Answer: that is true. A dollar in Mississippi takes you much further than a dollar in New York whether you are purchasing food, shelter, or service. But to concede this point is not to make the different point that the relative figures are meaningless. In fact, there *are* differences in standards of living, even after correcting for the purchasing value of the dollar, of such a character as to distinguish not only between Mississippi and New York, which rank number fifty and number one, but between Vermont and Wisconsin, which rank thirty-second and twenty-seventh. And anyway, people who lean too heavily on the argument that relative differences in standard of living tend to dissipate when one takes into account the purchasing power of the dollar, and also intangible benefits such as unpolluted air, uncrowded living conditions, the absent temptations of costly urban distractions, and so on, can all too easily talk themselves into saying that, adjusted, the standard of living in Mississippi is equal to the standard of living in New York, in which

case there would be no role left to play for federal redistributionists at all, unless they wanted to import Mississippi air into New York, and export *Last Tango in Paris* to Mississippi.

2. It is observed that there are subtle fluctuations in state and federal tax policies, depending on whether the state desires to overcome a tendency by the federal government towards progressivity, or whether the state intends to accentuate this progressivity. That is true, even as it is true that the federal government goes in for regressive taxation, for instance in excise taxes on staples and in payroll taxes. These matters will be touched on more extensively in the chapter on tax reform. For these purposes one need only accost the argument that although it is true that the federal government typically finds itself sending back to the states whence it took the money most of the money it took—we have seen that only 9 percent of the grants-in-aid and revenue sharing was effectively redistributed to the nineteen poorer states—in fact *different* people in a given state get the money, back from Washington, from those who sent the money to Washington.

It is, of course, at this stage that one needs to ask, rather humorlessly, the critical question. Is it the understanding of those who defend the existing system that the state is, or ought to be, nothing more than a civil abstraction? The state of Rhode Island sends to Washington, in taxes, $28,790,000 and gets back $29,070,000. a. Although there is a slight (1 percent) surplus, what would the surplus have come to if the transaction had been relieved of the federal carrying cost? b. In a democratic situation, particularly one which has regularly identified the voters of Rhode Island as in favor of federal welfare, what are the reasons for supposing that if the voters of Rhode Island are willing to tax from one set

of Rhode Islanders for the benefit of a different set of
Rhode Islanders, they will only consent to do so if their
money is routed from the first party to the second via
Washington rather than via Providence?

Surely much is to be gained from encouraging the
individual states to test individual approaches to various
problems of welfare. California has been attempting
reforms, but is hamstrung by the long shadow of Washington, intimidated by the possibility of losing money it
might collect from HEW, frightened at the possibility of
being handled by the courts as New York State was
handled. Still it is trying, and other states will profit from
its experiences. But the profit would be greater if the
burdens were lighter.

And, anyway, isn't it reasonable to suppose that in a
country of 200 million people, of diverse interests and
predilections, occupying an area as large as our own,
some states would wish to emphasize different kinds of
aid? Florida, for very good reasons, is more concerned
with the aged than, say, Oregon. New York is more
concerned with the ghetto than, say, Idaho. Some states,
for the sake of educational prestige, will bid vast sums of
money for big-name scholars: that, surely, is their
business, but it is unreasonable to tax other states for
these ornaments.

The evolution of federal policy is clearly towards
influencing the direction and intensity of state taxation.
This is effected precisely by the device of the grant-in-
aid. The formal authority, at least under existing constitutional understanding, remains with the state to reject
federal grants-in-aid which are proffered to supplement
state welfare appropriations. It is obvious that that kind
of independence is not often asserted. One commentator
recently observed that if Congress were to adopt legislation to contribute 90 percent of the cost of erecting

gold-plated polygons in public parks, inevitably gold-plated polygons would appear in every public park in the United States. Thus Mississippi, with the lowest per capita income in the United States, taxes its citizens $170 out of every thousand dollars of personal income, compared to New York's $170.30. One necessarily deduces from the figures, which indicate a far heavier internal tax burden on Mississippians than New Yorkers, given the huge difference in their income, either that Mississippi is far gone in an unadvertised internal socialism; or that Mississippi is pursuing federal tax dollars. Those who take the macrocosmic view are not very interested in what or who was responsible for imposing the proximate pressure on Mississippi to do the right thing. The procedure-suspending point is altogether defensible but is, of course, incompatible with democratic practice, and with the axiomatic right of the people to—know.

In a previous book I decocted two laws from the operation of liberal economic doctrine. The first is that the public is trained to assume that *the dollar that issues out of Washington, D.C., is spontaneously generated.* Illustrations are abundant. There exists, no doubt, the politician who has attempted to make his way in one of the wealthier states by instructing his constituents in the net economic disadvantages to them of welfare enterprises which the candidate nevertheless espouses; but nobody remembers his name. Do we infer from this that if the proposed reform were enacted, subsidies from the wealthier states to the poorer states would terminate? That, strangely, is the misanthropic conclusion. The sum of money necessary to help those states that need help turns out to be so small as to make it plausible that those who talk about the idealism of democracy might practice that idealism even if they are permitted to understand the workings of it.

The second generality I arrived at is that, under liberal economic doctrine, it is held that *the dollar is virtuously deployed as the distance increases between where it is collected and where it is spent.* The two laws, if they can presume to that station, touch upon each other, supported as they are by a common ignorance. The most parochial issues are the most illuminating. The subways of New York City are in crisis, and although the dollar depreciated by only 24 percent between the time Mr. Lindsay was elected mayor in 1965 and the time he left office in 1973, it was projected that the cost of a subway fare would need to rise from the 15 cents it cost in 1965 to 60 cents, i.e., by 400 percent. Leaving aside entirely any matter of mismanagement, it was not questioned in New York City by any of the mayoralty candidates to succeed Lindsay that a) subsidies for the subways by the municipal government are desirable; that b) subsidies for the subways by the state government are more desirable; and that c) subsidies for the subways by the federal government are still more desirable. We have seen that, by great ingenuity and cunning, New York has recently managed to obtain, net, subsidies from such states as Missouri and Virginia. But even if it were documented in a statement signed by Price, Waterhouse, the ACLU, the Consumers Union, Ralph Nader, and the Economics Departments of all the New York City colleges, that if the four and a half million subway riders themselves shouldered the entire cost of operating the subways, they would be net better off in the long run than if the cost were assumed by (a) City Hall, (b) Albany, or (c) Washington, the people, reared on liberal economic doctrine, would not believe. Blessed are they who do not see yet believe. It will take time to instruct people in economic truths, but the effort is worth it. For one thing, the benefits are palpable. For another, we have not very much time left in which to vindicate the democratic idea. The young generation is already dangerously close to concluding that the whole thing is eyewash, and that no one cares to tell them the truth. They are very nearly correct.

CHAPTER II

Taxation

Towards a Simplified Tax

SECTION 509 of the Internal Revenue Code instructs us as follows. "For purposes of paragraph 3, an organization described in paragraph 2 shall be deemed to include an organization described in section 501 c, sub-paragraphs 4, 5 or 6; which would be described in paragraph 2 if it were an organization described in section 501 c 3." With such ventures in lucidity the 1969 Tax Reform Law was launched.

Not long after that, a middle-class resident of Atlanta, Georgia, took his modest ledger to an IRS taxpayer assistance office in Atlanta and asked for help in filling out the tax form so that he might calculate his net situation. Having got back the completed form, he was apparently dissatisfied with the "bottom line," a term in accounting so graphic it has lately taken off as a metaphor ("Hamlet's bottom line was against suicide"). So he consulted another IRS officer in Rome, Georgia, presenting him with the identical raw material. That consultant weighed in with a figure of tax due substantially different from the previous figure. Intrigued by the discrepancy, he took his case to a third IRS man in Des Moines, Iowa. Once again the figure was significantly different.

I take it that at this point our hero was pricked less by curiosity about his indebtedness than about the lengths his evolving experience would take him to, because he went on to consult two more professionals, without damaging his record: no two of them agreed on how much money was owed. At this point he gave the story to the *Wall Street Journal,* and it is not known whether the expenses he incurred were listed as deductible, or even if he had to consult a sixth on the question.

In any event, a front-page story resulted. Many readers were reminded of what they had already numbly discovered for themselves, namely that the tax laws are, in respect of economic subtleties, ambiguous, not to say inscrutable. The layman has no alternative than to read the law impressionistically, particularly if he is giving it a political reading ("It favors the rich!" "It takes no realistic notice of the need to retool!"). If professionals cannot come to the same conclusion as to what the code says, it is not surprising—the incidence of the new tax law on rich and poor quite apart—that the call for tax reform should have attracted support even from Americans who had no use for George McGovern, who made reforms a staple of his program. The rate schedule aside, the exemptions, deductions, depreciations aside, there is the sheer complexity of it for those millions (approximately 76, i.e., 42 percent of those who pay a federal tax) who, even if they finally elect to take the standard exemptions, are nevertheless driven to calculating the alternative, and this requires itemizing all deductions, in order to ascertain by which method they are better off. And for the other millions who fill out the short form prayerfully, tearfully, there is the torment of wondering whether they took full advantage of every possibility. The unexhausted, and the semiexhausted, are beginning to ask the question: Why? Why should it be so complicated?

The reason why is that tax reforms seek to improve on previous tax reforms by arching their provisions, like jungle leaves writhing for the sunlight, towards such rays of justice and equity as are discernible at any given moment of relative composure in American politics, when the pandemonium freezes, as for a photographer, for just long enough to permit one set of claimants to overshadow another. Thus a tax reform is born. For that brief moment we have a new code that is taken as an expression of social policy. It is an assertion of justice, justice understood as a blend of considerations: the necessities of the state; the toleration of the body politic; the relationships of power among the affected interests; and rough justice.

Our tax laws were designed historically to raise revenue for the operations of government. Along the way the operations of government inflated in purpose and ambition, evolving from modest Jeffersonian instruments for effecting the safety of the state into the gargantuan instruments of the social perfectionists. Accordingly the tax law became something other than a mere revenue-raising instrument. Sometimes the purpose of the tax law is unsmilingly direct, sometimes it is oblique. Donations to hospitals and churches are ruled to be tax deductible, for no reason more complicated than the desire to aid hospitals and churches. Interest payments to mortgage companies by homeowners are deductible, not in order to aid mortgage companies, or even the homeowners exclusively, but indirectly to encourage homeownership: that institution of social stability that induces people to sink their roots in a community, raise a family there, patron-

ize the schools and the churches, pay taxes, and make
known their political preferences, preferably for the
incumbents.

The difficulty is that any attempt to make justice
through the tax code not only tends to fail to effect the
justice intended—for instance, by imposing unforeseen
penalties on the very class of people one is attempting to
help—but tends to effect a fresh injustice—by imposing
unforeseen penalties on another class of people one had
no intention of hurting. An example is the so-called split
income taxpayer.

The federal income tax became a significant social
factor with the advent of the Second World War. True,
the rates had risen very sharply for a little while during
the masochistic enthusiasm of the First World War. But
by the late thirties there were only 3 million people who
paid federal income taxes, the rest being exempt by
virtue of the schedule of exclusions. The World War II
tax raised the number of taxpayers to the unprecedented
figure of 42 million. And, as had been the case since
1913, there was only the one tax rate per income level. It
did not matter whether you were a single wage earner or
the working member of a married couple: you paid taxes
at the identical rate.

But after the war there was a dawning recognition of
the practical uses of the community property law. Six
states of the Union had such a law, and residents of these
states began to assert their claims vis-à-vis Internal
Revenue. What they said was that inasmuch as under the
state law that governed them the wife was entitled to
one-half the husband's income, then that one-half was
never his in any taxable sense. This meant (to speak for
convenience' sake of the husband as the wage earner and
the wife as the non-wage earner) that a husband earning
$20,000 per year had only to pay federal taxes on

$10,000. Granted, the wife would then need to pay taxes on $10,000. But, under the progressive rubric, the sum of the parts is not equal to, rather is substantially less than, the whole. Internal Revenue, sensing the danger in reduced revenues, fought hard to protect its turf. But the Supreme Court ruled that the predatory concerns of the upstart Internal Revenue Service did not supersede the venerable traditions of the six states in question, which inherited their notions of community property from Spanish and French custom.

The advantages of married couples in the six states having been affirmed, they were rapidly advertised, and state legislatures elsewhere began to explore proposals to convert their own systems into community property for the sole purpose of getting in on the advantages that now accrued to married people only in the six privileged states.

Meanwhile pressure on Congress was coming in tangentially. In 1942 a law had innocently passed allowing a previously married man to deduct, for the purpose of computing his tax, any money now paid in alimony to his former wife. That seemed fair. But suddenly married couples discovered that Congress had made divorce profitable. Paying taxes separately, a divorced couple paid less than when married. In the pragmatic spirit of America couples were being tempted to live together luxuriously in sin rather than parsimoniously in wedlock. Congress did not like that.

And so, to do something on this score and to avert the stampede to convert to community property, Congress reluctantly acted—by extending to married couples everywhere the right to split their income. I say reluctantly because Congress had been warned about the loss in revenue that the universalization of split income would bring. That Congress regretted. On the other hand, it was glad for the occasion to express itself as being in favor of the institution of the family, and as not insensible to the extra costs of raising a family, costs which are not, as a rule, part of the burden of the single taxpayer.

Then in 1951 Congress discreetly recognized the category of the unmarried head of a household. What to do about unmarried parents of dependents? Congress decided to give such persons *half* the advantage of a joint return by married persons. Sin should cost *something*.

All of this went smoothly except that in due course the single taxpayers developed a class consciousness and began to ask why *they* were being discriminated against. In tax law it tends to be truer than ever that to favor somebody is almost necessarily to discriminate against somebody else. Lobbyists for the single taxpayer made their points persuasively. Individual taxpayers at the higher brackets found themselves paying as much as 42 percent more, on identical income, than married couples. Why is it the business of Congress, they asked, to penalize bachelorhood and spinsterhood? And to do so, moreover, at one and the same time that Congress is fussing over the population explosion?

When the Tax Reform Act of 1969 came along, Congress, weakened by the arguments of the single taxpayers and no doubt influenced by the imminent enfranchisement of Americans between the ages of eighteen and twenty-one, most of whom would vote the first time or two as unmarried wage earners, decided to compromise. So the new law ruled that no single taxpayer in the same bracket as a married taxpayer could be made to pay to the government in tax more-than-20-percent-more than a married taxpayer in the same bracket.

This by no means appeased the single taxpayers, who redoubled their demand for absolute parity. Whereupon the beleaguered Congress began to hear the cannon of a brand-new enemy, created by fission out of the tax reform law. The latest afflicted class (to be discovered) is the husband and wife who both work *and* earn a middle-to-high income. *They* discovered that they now had to pay 19 percent more in taxes than if they were divorced or living together unmarried. A lobby for their relief has of course been born. A bill has been introduced (but does not yet appear to have got anywhere) which specifies, blearily, that no married taxpayer should be taxed more than if he were single. If such a bill is passed, the married person would presumably figure out his tax in his civil capacity as 50 percent of a couple. Then he would figure out his tax as if he were single and pay the lesser figure. Meanwhile yet another bill has been introduced in behalf of the unmarried, childless taxpayer. That bill says simply that no single taxpayer should be made to pay more tax than he would pay if he were married. That taxpayer, assuming the bill were passed, would figure out his tax as a single person, then figure out his tax as if he were married and pay the lesser figure.

Presumably if both these bills were passed, a few weeks or months would go by after which married couples would begin to lobby Congress to take into realistic account the cost of bringing up children. On this matter, as it happens, Congress is extremely vulnerable. The cost of bringing up a child, translated into an exemption, was set at $600 in 1948. There it stood until the 1969 Act which programmed it to rise in stages to $750 in 1972. Ironically, the single person's exemption, which was also allowed to rise to $750 in 1972, began at $3,000 way back in 1913. In 1913 dollars, that meant roughly that no unmarried vice-presidents of medium companies needed to pay any tax at all. The World War I fever collapsed that exemption to $1,000. It had slid down to $500 by

World War II, after which it was raised, in deference to the great postwar inflation, to the $600 where it stood for twenty-one years.

Now if the 1969 law had adjusted it on the World War II base, the exemption would have increased not to $750, but to $1,150, the dollar during that period having inflated by 130 percent. However, if Congress had acted thus reasonably, two things would have resulted, one of them tangible, the other less so.

—An increase of every hundred dollars in the general exemption means the loss of $4 billion in federal revenue. Thus raising the exemption from $750 to $1,150 would have meant an additional loss of revenue to the federal government of over $16 billion. That is a lot of money to lose, particularly when one is running deficits of over twice that figure.

—And the intangible loss is the millions of taxpayers who drop altogether from the rolls. And this is a worrisome development in a democracy that does not disfranchise nontaxpayers. The dangers are obvious. People who do not pay any tax at all are insouciant about other people's taxation and are more easily convinced that munificent social services are easily financed by the simple expedient of raising taxes. Indeed there is the argument that everyone, no matter how poor, should pay a tax—however paradoxical the picture of the man stopping first at the welfare window and then at the income tax window; a paradox, however, that we learned to live with shortly after the war on poverty was launched.

Of course the poorest people do pay taxes—excise, and payroll, and sales taxes in particular. But these taxes are virtually invisible. The withholding tax was, in part, an effort at immaterialization, but it has not been altogether successful. Too many taxpayers, struggling over their forms, engage the reality of the federal tax. And too many of them experience it when, by itemizing their deductions, they find themselves entitled to a refund. And when, by taking supplementary income into account, they find themselves, in the spring, owing money. In short, even the device of the withholding tax has not altogether anesthetized taxpayers to the pain of paying taxes. The argument is that to eliminate millions of taxpayers would not only reduce the tax base beyond the 49.8 percent where it now stands, but release people from a ritual that harnesses them, however lightly, to the economic experience of government.

But consider now the anfractuosity of tax policy, taking into account only a generation's experience with a single category of exemptions. The narrative would appear to be as follows.

1. Congress decides (let us omit the wild oscillations before World War II) that a wage earner should not be taxed for income he clearly needs in order to provide himself, his wife, and his children with the bare necessities of subsistence. According to this view "taxable income" is only surplus income. If you need $2 a day in order to live, then taxation begins with $2.01.

2. But Congress begins immediately to cheat on its own premises because of tangential considerations. For one thing, it simply ignores the depreciation of the dollar, permitting the exemption to stand at the same figure over a period during which the dollar depreciates by 130 percent. Moreover, Congress simply ignores the theoretical definition of taxable income when the income tax is itself calculated. In theory, taxable income should be calculated after taxes are deducted. This rule is observed by permitting the taxpayer to reduce his taxable income by the sum of money paid in (most) state and local taxes.

But it is grandly ignored in respect of federal taxes. A man with a taxable income of $20,000 who has to pay, say, $4,000 to the federal government as a function of the $20,000 is being cheated. From the $20,000 of taxable income should be subtracted the sum of money the federal government proposes to tax him. That is his disposable income. His taxable income. The federal government profiteers by a few percentage points by ignoring the distinction.

3. Congress, facing an epidemic of community tax laws, yields—intending to confer advantages impartially to married couples wherever they live.

4. Nonmarried couples object, so Congress compromises, extending benefits to them.

5. Single taxpayers object. Congress compromises, extending benefits to them.

6. Married taxpayers object, pointing out a net discrimination against certain of their number.

7. Single taxpayers are unsatisfied, pointing to their residual disadvantages.

8. Married taxpayers are dissatisfied, pointing out the economic unreality of an exemption unharnessed to the inflation of the dollar.

❦

A proposed reform:

Congress should eliminate the progressive feature of the income tax.

Congress should eliminate all deductions except those that relate directly to the cost of acquiring income.

Congress should eliminate all exemptions.

Congress should eliminate the corporation tax.

Congress should reimburse taxpayers below the poverty line any federal taxes regressive in impact.

Congress should levy a uniform tax of 15 percent on all income.

Congress should assist people in the poorer states who live below the poverty level. (See Chapter I.)

Congress should collect income tax revenues in behalf of the individual states, at whatever rates are specified by the states.

In his great book, *Constitution of Liberty,* Professor Friedrich Hayek reaches the point where he has to say it or undermine all that went before. Since he cannot tell a lie, he confesses that, notwithstanding what he knows it will cost him, he must renounce the progressive income tax. He does so in a chapter rich in analysis and scholarship, with subtle, and thoughtful, hedges. But even after he has made his great demonstration, the pages are tear-stained, because he knows that he has run the risk of losing his audience, which as a matter of fact he did, though perhaps he had lost it before. Hayek's masterpiece is the kind of book born to be rediscovered.

It is twenty years since *The Uneasy Case for Progressive Taxation,* by Walter Blum and Harry Karlaven, was published, uneasily, and as many years since Bertrand de Jouvenel published his distinguished lectures on *The Ethics of Redistribution.* Even so, critics of progressive income taxation make their points self-consciously, defensively.

Progressive income taxation, in the measured words of Hayek, is "the chief source of irresponsibility of democratic action [and] the crucial issue on which the whole character of future society will depend." The idea is not particularly productive economically (the yield is surprisingly small since 91 percent of all taxable income is in brackets of less than $10,000), it is hostile to the ideal of a classless society (the wealthier are a class apart, treated differently under the law), and it is the greatest cause of the misallocation of economic energy since the discovery

" So far as federal income taxes are concerned, the U.S. tax system has always been reasonably progressive—and it became more so with the Tax Reform Act of 1969. The act, as the chart below makes plain, increased federal income taxes for the rich and decreased them for everybody else. (Data are from studies by Joseph A. Pechman of the Brookings Institution; the percentages refer to all money income, whether taxable under present law or not, plus realized capital gains.)

But the U.S. tax system as a whole is not so progressive, as the chart at the right also makes plain. The chart, which shows that the lowest tax rate is paid at the middle-income levels, is based on an ambitious study of 1968 incomes and taxes made by Herman Miller and Roger Herriot of the U.S. Census Bureau. The "income" used in their calculations includes some imputed items, such as the rental value of owner-occupied housing. Miller and Herriot assume that property taxes are shifted to renters and that two-thirds of the corporation tax is ultimately paid by shareholders, while one-third is passed on in the form of higher prices. "

Reprinted by permission
from *Fortune*, December 1972.

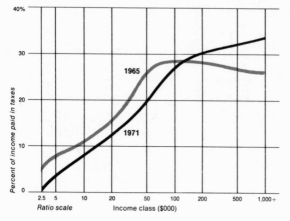

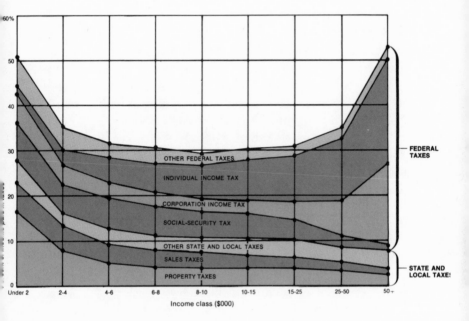

60% |

50 |

40 |

30 | OTHER FEDERAL TAXES

INDIVIDUAL INCOME TAX

20 | CORPORATION INCOME TAX

SOCIAL-SECURITY TAX

10 | OTHER STATE AND LOCAL TAXES

SALES TAXES

PROPERTY TAXES

0 |

Under 2   2-4   4-6   6-8   8-10   10-15   15-25   25-50   50+

Income class ($000)

FEDERAL TAXES

STATE AND LOCAL TAXES

of the marketplace. (It is idle to speculate on how many dollars are torturedly spent by people and enterprises attempting to mitigate the steepening incline of progressive taxation, but fractious to suppose that it comes to less than tens of billions of dollars.) Having said as much, I give it as my opinion (elaborated below) that the individual states should not be barred (a constitutional amendment would be the only way to do it) from experimenting with progressive income taxation.

It is generally held to be idle to put forward a figure absolutely, beyond which the federal government should not be permitted to tax—the doctrine of the inflexible limit is too easily collapsed by invoking National Emergency. The alleged debt ceiling periodically set by Congress is a piffle. Yet it is useful to arrange one's arguments around a fixed figure, whatever the escape clauses. And anyway, it is in the American tradition to argue a posteriori, from the particular to the general: How has the present system worked?

Professor Hayek triumphantly reveals what most students of taxation have come, in the interim since his book's publication, to accept as a commonplace: namely, that although there are episodic efforts at direct subventions of the very poor, nevertheless in democratic societies the incidence of taxation falls regressively, and has over the years almost everywhere in the world, on the poorer rather than the middle income classes, the latter having the principal leverage in democratic bourgeois societies; and then rises for the upper income class whose political leverage is relatively slight. This is so in part because of the intractability of tax policy as agent of social policy; in part—as we say—because of the power of the middle class; and in part because of the technology of tax collection. The property tax, the excise tax, the sales tax, and the Social Security tax are the principal instruments of effectively regressive taxation, but these taxes are not easily redesigned so as to relieve the poor. *Fortune* magazine published a graph in December, 1972, making the point—graphically. See above.

The second of the two graphs shows that although taxes (in 1968) took more than 50 percent of the income of those who earn under $2,000 per year, they took only (only!) 30 percent of the income of those in the $8,000–$10,000 level. The poor man's taxes, manifestly, are regressive in effect, certainly not in intention. The impoverished cigarette addict who pays half the cost of a pack of cigarettes in federal and state excise and sales taxes and the smoker and the nonsmoker alike, who pay to the community a property tax on their apartment or house, is not the intended target of the tax laws, but he is no less surely the victim of them, and any effort, to his advantage, to restore proportionality—which is to be distinguished from an effort to institute progressivity—does not compromise the admirable principles this essay seeks to serve.

Assuming that 30 percent were the stipulated rate of federal, state, and local taxation, one might, in pursuit of proportionality, reasonably return the difference between 50 and 30 percent—i.e., 20 percent—to the $2,000 earner. That comes to $400. The figure appears exiguous. It is, however, useful to remember that (a) $400, for someone earning $2,000, is not an inconsequential sum of money; and (b) the figure is over five times the redistributionist advantage ($75) currently being given, per capita, to the poorer states by the entire complex of federal grants-in-aid and revenue sharing.

This essay seeks to argue the usefulness and the vitality of the federal system and, accordingly, to encourage the states in coping resourcefully with the anomalies.

One should reject, under the circumstances, any

suggestion that the federal government casually reimburse all those who are shortchanged by the tax system insofar as the individual states, through their own tax laws, are responsible. To do this would be to short-circuit the prudential and principled advances attempted by this analysis. The federal government's intercession must be in behalf only of the poorer states and compensatory only as regards victims of its own tax policies.

It is—granted—the federal government that imposes some of the regressive taxes, most prominently the Social Security tax. But—see the chart above—the most arduously regressive taxes are state taxes. It is up to the states to devise the means of compensating for them. There are more than a few imaginative ways to do this, and there are more than a few states, some of them imaginative.

While granting Hayek's point, and also that the level of taxation might need to rise in time of great national need, there is no reason to avoid making the workaday proposal. To wit, a tax by the federal government of 15 percent. On all personal income. No more exemptions, deductions, exclusions, credits, preferences. No more *exemptions*? To quote General Nathan Bedford Forrest, I told you twicet, goddammit, no.

Since Taxable Income is only one-half (49.8%) of Personal Income, a straight 15 percent on all Personal Income would yield to the government 134 percent of what it took in under the present system. If, as George McGovern's advisers plausibly argued in 1972, one accepts 15 percent of Personal Income as nontaxable by any defensible criterion (e.g., the actual cost of doing business—the traveling salesman deducting what he paid for gasoline), then at the 15 percent rate, taxes would bring in 114.1 percent ($102.7 billion) of what they brought in in 1970 ($90.4 billion).

In 1970, Congress raised $35 billion from the corporation tax. Added to the $90.4 billion from personal income taxes, that came to $125.4 billion. But since we propose to do away altogether with the corporation tax, we see that government revenues under the 15 percent plan might have fallen $22.7 billion short of the actual figures for 1970. (Actually, much of the corporate income would now be taxed as increased stockholder income, but let that go for the moment.) We have also seen (in Chapter I) that by concerning itself with the welfare problems of only the poorer states, the federal government would reduce its needs by over $25 billion, leaving it, on this showing alone, with a surplus of about $2.5 billion, enough to substantially reimburse taxpayers below the poverty line for their burden in regressive federal taxes.

The theoretical case against progressive income taxation does not evaporate as one moves down from the central government to lower units of government. But however obnoxious it remains philosophically, the practical argument weakens insofar as the progressive tax can be avoided without forfeiture of citizenship by those who believe themselves victimized insufferably.

The point is made in order to stress the escape-valve aspect of progressive and even confiscatory tax laws when leveled by individual states. One *can* leave a state, and thus counter-pressures against intolerable taxation are generated. Anthony Burgess left England on the grounds that he thought English tax laws sadistic, and came to the United States, suggesting that he is inured to lesser forms of sadism: but he maintains his English citizenship. Noel Coward, on leaving England to take up residence in Switzerland a dozen years ago for the obvious purpose of avoiding a 98 percent tax, was met by the press at the airport in Geneva. Why, asked a reporter, was he leaving England to live in Switzerland? "Devoted to chocolates," he replied.

One accepts the advantages of the Burgesses of this world and the Cowards. They are, relatively, wealthy and mobile. The country that permits its Burgesses to escape very high taxation yet still retain citizenship should worry less about closing the loophole for the Burgesses than opening a loophole for the sub-Burgesses. The federal composition of the United States is ideal for making this possible, though it must not be assumed that only very large countries can indulge internal competition among taxing authorities. Switzerland, for instance, does it.

It is, I am saying, one thing for New York State, or California, or Illinois, to experiment with very high progressive taxation, another for the federal government to do it. This essay is about the uses of simplicity, directness, procedure, and about the value to a society of prudent experimentation. Such experimentation can only be done by individual states. To experiment nationally is to run a risk of great strategic misadventure. To decline to run such risks induces a social stodginess, or else reforms so hedged in with qualifications as to come out sounding like the 1969 tax law.

If the state of New York, or California, should elect to continue their progressive tax schedules, let them do so—cautiously, experimentally, with an eye to the effect of it. Perhaps such states would want, on adoption by the federal government of a universal rate, to steepen the progressive rate and to make other adjustments designed to reverse regressive taxes. Presumably they would elect to take on many of the welfare burdens formerly undertaken by the federal government.

On one point only should the states coordinate with the federal government, and that is the matter of collection. Economists have pointed out that the federal Internal Revenue System is marvelously efficient, which is true, an extension of the principle that the knowledge one is going to be hanged in a fortnight concentrates the mind wonderfully as well of the taxpayer as of the murderer. The states should avail themselves of the apparatus of Internal Revenue—not merely for the sake of economy, but in order to spare taxpayers the requirement of calculating twice, often with reference to wholly unrelated standards, the sums of money owed, first to the federal government, then to their own states.

Internal Revenue should agree to collect the taxes decreed by the states. The tax form would include a column of figures appropriate to the state in which the taxpayer lives. If the tax due to the federal government is (say) $1,480, the taxpayer would run his finger across to see how much his state is asking someone whose taxable income at 15 percent is $1,480. Suppose the figure to be $911. The taxpayer encloses two checks, one made out to U.S. Internal Revenue for the first figure, the second to (say) the State of Illinois for the second. IRS collects the Illinois money and remits it to Springfield, charging a small service fee infinitely less than is needed to maintain an entire paraphernalia of income tax collection in Illinois.

If Congress were to eliminate the business tax altogether, what would happen? It is typical that no one quite knows. Some experts maintain that the business tax is a wholly regressive tax, that as a cost of doing business it is entirely passed along to the consumer, and that since the average consumer needs to spend a greater amount of his income than the average shareholder, the tax is regressive. Two researchers in the Census Bureau disagree. They conclude, after a complicated examination of the situation, that two-thirds of the tax is, in fact, shouldered by the shareholders, who are, for the most part, in the middle and upper income brackets, and one-third by the consumers. It is—once again—instructive that no one knows what the impact actually is of a tax designed primarily (a) to be popular, in cultivation of the superstition that that which is paid by General Motors to the government, or by the Chase Manhattan Bank, doesn't really count, and in any case is there more or less inexhaustibly; and (b) to provide Internal Revenue with, in effect, efficient tax-collecting subsidiaries. It is on the whole easier, Internal Revenue reckons, to collect a set percentage of General Motors' income than varying percentages of General Motors' income as passed along to 1,270,000 shareholders. But, of course, under the proposed reform the percentages would cease to vary: it would be 15 percent straight up and down the line.

As regards the argument over incidence, let us take the middle position between the experts and postulate that the corporation tax is now being paid one-half by shareholders, one-half by consumers. What would be the effect of eliminating the tax under the proposed reform?

As it stands, corporate business is paying 32 percent of its profits in federal tax. In theory, a company that earned $1.5 million a year (after taxes) before the proposed reform would suddenly find itself about to earn over $2 million. The value of the stock would, assuming the price-earnings ratio remained the same, rise in anticipation of the increased earnings. Let us, however, now assume, applying the 50-50 Rule, that competition forces half the bonanza to be passed along to the consumer in reduced prices. That would leave, net to the shareholder, a 15 percent (actually 16 percent) increase in the value of his stock. This is not the stuff of which social nightmares are made in sane societies—a reduction (varying with the cost to the supplier of the incremental unit) in the price of all products and services provided by

corporations, even in the knowledge that stock averages
will increase by 15 percent. (It is amusing to extend the
argument ad absurdum. If the price of all products and
services were reduced by 100 percent, would anyone
object to a 1000 percent increase in the value of the stock
market?) Over a five-month period in 1973 the market
decreased by over 17 percent. Such oscillations are
socially irrelevant, and certainly no reason for denying
major reforms aimed at coherence, symmetry, and an
end to hallucination.

Capital gains of course would be taxed as regular
income. And it would be reasonable to tax these gains
yearly. Companies that elected to plow profits into
development would be required to advise stockholders of
their undistributed earnings per share, on which a tax
would be due every year. The directors could, of course,
vote to pay 15 percent of their profits in behalf of the
stockholders. Capital losses should be fully deductible
against all forms of income.

It is not possible to predict by exactly how much
Internal Revenue would benefit from the increased
profits to shareholders and increased consumption
through lower prices. But the combination of increased
profits-distributed and consumption-increased would result in an augmentation of taxable income and, one can
safely assume, a multibillion dollar addition to federal
revenues.

Now on the assumption that in order to help the poor
states the government were to maintain a level of
assistance equal to that of 1970—the highest in history
up to that moment—Congress would need to channel to
the poor states the $2.8 billion net transfer payments
isolated in the preceding chapter, plus effective reim-
bursement to individuals in those nineteen states who,
though they live below the poverty level, pay in various

federal taxes more than 15 percent of their income to
Washington. The population of the nineteen states is 41.6
million. The number of people estimated to be living
below the poverty level nationally (1969 figures) is 27.25
million, or 14 percent (by the standard of the Bureau of
Labor Statistics, which is slightly different from that of
the Bureau of the Census). The figure climbs, for the
poorer states, to 21 percent (of the 41.6 million residents
of the poorer states), for a total of 8.8 million. Helping
these 8.8 million people is reasonably viewed as the
partial responsibility of the federal government, and it is
plain that there is ample money to do this even after
effecting these reforms.

These figures show an apparent disadvantage to the
lower income taxpayers as between the current and the
proposed system. It is perhaps the single most infuriating
aspect of the tax figures that they need to be distrusted
with religious fidelity.

Detailed analysis is not available after 1969. At that
point the new law came into effect, in its infinite
complexity. It did, however, reduce the tax burden on
the very poor, and increase it on the rich, and as such
was accepted as a Tax Reform with a Good Housekeeping label, until George McGovern sought to anathema-
tize it as protecting the rich by permitting loopholes to
survive. Leaving those charges aside, a few observations:

1. In 1968, after forty years of the welfare state,
Americans who earned $2,000 or less were paying over 50
percent of their income in taxes. State and local taxes
took 27.2 percent, or over one-half. The single heaviest
local tax (curiously) was the property tax, at 16.2
percent. Then the sales tax (6.6 percent), then miscella-
neous taxes. Federal taxes on the very poor amounted to
22.7 percent, of which the income tax amounted to only

1.2 percent, which is to say just over $20. The poor man's share of the corporate profit tax is calculated at 6 percent. That, the statisticians deduce, is the percentage of his income he is paying in higher prices because of the corporation tax. Researchers assign to the taxpayer of this bracket 7.6 percent as his Social Security tax, an intricate deduction one is better off taking on faith. That leaves 7.9 percent in miscellaneous taxes for which the federal government is responsible.

2. Transfer payments, i.e., payments of various kinds made by the government in behalf of someone at the expense of someone else, are made in behalf of this category of Americans, and the latest available figures are that they come to 106.5 percent, while the same group pays about 50 percent in various taxes.

3. The back-and-forth (take $826, give back $2,130) says something no more complicated than that under certain circumstances taxing authorities find it more convenient to figure out a way of paying out something to a taxpayer, than to figure out ways to exempt him from the payment of certain taxes. Those in the very lowest brackets whose taxes appear preposterously high are regular consumers of, e.g., gasoline, cigarettes, and alcohol, all of them high-taxed items by both the federal government and the states. But it is easier to charge the poor American the regular tax, at the filling station, at the vending machine, and at the liquor store, than to tattoo his exemption on his forehead and force the merchandisers to recalculate the cost of every item he buys. If businessmen tried to do that, they would be hauled off and charged with an offense called discriminatory pricing.

4. The practical point in favor of charging everyone the same price for a gallon of gasoline, even though half the cost of the gasoline is tax, extends psychically to the

income tax. Indigent Americans are first-class citizens in respect of civil liberties. They should pay taxes on their income even as they pay taxes on gasoline: like everyone else, for reasons less obviously necessary to the practical conduct of commerce, but no less obviously desirable in promoting a sense of civic equality.

5. We arrive then at the question: How should the federal government (with which we are dealing exclusively), in its struggle for proportionality, behave towards the lowest income brackets from which it is now expecting income tax payments at 15 percent? The answer, surely, is that the federal government should return to these income taxpayers money the government is taking from them through other taxes.

We have seen that the $2,000 taxpayer was paying (in 1968) 22.7 percent of his income in federal taxes. We desire that that figure should reduce comprehensively to 15 percent. (Social Security payments are obviously excluded.) The disappearance of the corporation tax will automatically reduce his tax by 6 percent. By that measure alone, the federal government cuts almost in half its tax burden of 15 percent on the poor. The government should return to all taxpayers below the poverty line, through a credit against the income tax, the estimated tax raised by miscellaneous measures regressive in impact, or, at the present reckoning, 8 percent (7.9 percent, exactly). The combination, by statistical felicity, adds up to 14 percent, a remission almost exactly the equal of the federal tax the poor are now paying. This is a commitment to the idea of proportionality. Transfer payments beyond that point would be paid, with the exception of Social Security and veterans' benefits, only to residents of the poorer nineteen states.

There we have it.

I remember an experience in Copenhagen a few years

ago. My son and I were being shown the city by a guide fervent in his appreciation of all things Danish. He liked to ask questions the answers to which, clearly antici- pated, would cue in one of his nationalistic cadenzas. This time it was: "What is the highest tax in America?" Seventy-seven percent, I answered. "Well," he said, cheeks glowing with pride, "here it is ninety-eight percent!" He made it sound like the high-water mark of Scandinavian achievement. Perhaps it is.

It is time for fresher insights, for the rediscovery of rule by law. And it is never too soon to muse on the pleasures of the simple tax, and the end to the grotesqueries of justice by taxation. The benefits are integral and inciden- tal. I like best the professor who said, "Hell, for fifteen percent I wouldn't even *bother* to cheat on my taxes!" And the obscurer benefits. Lowering the tax on interest earned through savings, while eliminating the deduction on interest through borrowing, means that the incentive to save would rise substantially, and with it the supply of capital for housing, rapid transit, pollution control. Many special interest groups would disperse. Lobbying or bribing Congressmen to enact special tax legislation would no longer be worth their trouble and time. The inherently unfair treatment given to income bunched in only a few years—as with actors, writers, athletes, for instance—would suddenly cease to be a problem requir- ing fitful averaging schemes. But the greatest benefit is not so easily demonstrated. It is the pursuit of genuine equality before the law, and the pursuit of a democratic order based on an ongoing public awareness of economics and the public purpose.

CHAPTER III

Education

Towards Noncoerced Education

O F all the dreams of American liberalism, the dream that featured education—as the solvent of universal equality, harmony, and prosperity—was the most rudely shattered in the postwar decades. There had been the intuitive misgivings of such as Albert Jay Nock, whose resonant little lectures delivered at the University of Virginia in the thirties were (a) mostly unread, and (b) altogether disregarded by those few who read them—disregarded as the work of an elitist whose attachment to Jeffersonian democracy really boiled down to an attachment to Jefferson, rather than to democracy. Nock said that the mass of any people anywhere are uneducable, in his, and the traditional, sense of the word, that it makes sense for a free society to concern itself rather with the *training* of its citizens, and that it is very important not to confuse training with education because to confuse the terminology is to run the risk of confusing the substance. A few years after Nock delivered the Page Barbour lectures, enrollment in U.S. colleges and universities began its stupendous growth. In 1940, 16 percent of Americans of college age were matriculating at college. In 1970, the figure was 44 percent. Moreover, it wasn't only the white majority who were going to college. Far more American Negroes, as a percentage of the college-age population (13 percent), are now attending college, than British (8 percent), or French (10 percent).

As for secondary schools, education has become pretty much universal. In 1970, 90 percent of white children attended high school, and the figure for Negro children was almost as high (89 percent). The enthusiasm for education was such that in the two decades after the Second World War, money spent on education went up four and one-half times as fast as the gross national product. In adjusted dollars, the pay given to teachers rose 68 percent, twice as fast as wages in the private economy. By 1970 total expenditures for education were $77.6 billion—8 percent of the GNP, as compared with 2 percent in 1945.

In those happy days it was quite universally assumed that good education was something one got by spending money—the more dollars spent per student, the better the student's education. "Every empirical study of the relationship between expenditure level and quality of education adds its bit to the presumption that the relationship is strong," Professor Paul R. Mort of Teachers College, Columbia, had written in 1952 in his study on "Cost-Quality Relationship in Education."

"Studies of the relationship in acceptably organized districts suggest that schools that spend more, contribute more to the lifelong personal happiness of their charges and to the social and economic strength of Americans as a people."

Apart from the diffuser claims of education so grandly stated by Professor Mort, there were claims more concretely stated, for instance faith in education as the great unifier of the races. In 1954 the Supreme Court declared with a crackle of Old Testament thunder in its voice that

compulsory segregation in the schools was unconstitutional because sociological studies proved that separate
schooling was inherently unequal and had the effect of
denying, without due process, advantages to the victims
of segregation which they would not be without in
normal, i.e., integrated, circumstances. The civil rights
movement issued from this magna carta, and ten years
later at a great rally in Washington reached the apogee
of its idealism when the Reverend Martin Luther King
spoke of the dreams he dreamed. In quick succession the
measures demanded by the civil rights activists were
written into law. Early in 1973, ten years after the rally,
two researchers of liberal tendency were proudly reciting
the great economic achievements of the Negro people
during the preceding decade, and wondering plaintively
why these achievements had not been more widely
celebrated by Negro leaders. Messrs. Scammon and
Wattenberg took it for granted that the undeniable
economic progress of the Negro people was the result
primarily of the civil rights measures, and perhaps the
reason they took this for granted was precisely that it
could not be established. That, for instance, there had
been a causal relation between the end of Jim Crow in
Southern motels and the rise in Negro income; or
between the enfranchisement of the Negro voter in the
South and the graduation into the middle class of a
majority of the Negro people. On the point concerning
which there had been the closest study, there was no
progress at all to report. The 1964 Civil Rights Act had
almost offhandedly commissioned an investigation the
purpose of which was forever to document historically
that there was a difference between the quality of
education as administered to black children and to white
children, quality being defined in almost any way one
chose. The study was executed under the supervision of a

scholar who was parti pris to the thesis he set out to confirm. But when the figures came in, they were so scandalously, so iconoclastically disruptive of the governing assumptions that they were furtively released by the Office of Education over the Fourth of July weekend in 1966, pursuant to the doctrine of the public relations set that nothing released on a day so much given over to fleshly pursuits is likely to be given much thought. But the Coleman Report did get attention—slowly, as though on the Fourth of July a little firecracker had been set off at the beginning end of a very long fuse which, though it has set off many explosions, is still firing away. First there was a big study to study the Coleman Report, and there are now studies to study the studies of the Coleman Report, in saecula saeculorum. Coleman's findings are various, some of them lapidary, others merely suggestive, and before long Coleman was himself writing letters to the New York *Times* questioning some of his exegetes. But the word was in, and would never again be challenged with the old robustness with which the gentlemen of Teachers College used to instruct the community on the Cost-Quality Relationship in Education. The word: that (a) even in 1965 there was no significant disparity in the quality of education as administered to black and to white children; that (b) there was no significant correlation between the educational achievement of children on whom many dollars are spent and the achievement of children on whom fewer dollars are spent; and that (c) educational achievement depends on family background far more than on educational quality.

Other scholars took it from there. Arthur Jensen of Berkeley found, following his own communion with the figures, that differences in IQ on which educational achievement largely depends are, on the evidence, overwhelmingly genetic, i.e., inherited and fixed at birth.

Herrnstein deduced from this fact that differences of intelligence are substantially inherited rather than environmentally produced, that greater equality of opportunity would increase differences in achievement ultimately to lead to a meritocratic society with great differences in status and income which would be, largely, inherited. David Armor of Harvard, studying the effects of busing, concluded that the experiment had not enhanced the quality of education for black or white, had not increased ambition but had the opposite effect, did not diminish but rather increased racial self-consciousness, and retarded effective social relations between the races. Christopher Jencks, also of Harvard, then came along with a prodigious study the effect of which was to show that educational training had precious little to do with economic success in later years, puncturing yet another liberal assumption. Mr. Jencks, a devoted egalitarian, was so depressed by his own findings as to march uninterrupted, and one might say uninvited, into a series of proposals unrelated to his field of inquiry, advocating massive redistribution on the resigned and anti-historical assumption that otherwise the poor will not themselves advance economically. He advanced a novel argument for luxurious educational facilities. The best reason for expensive playgrounds and such in the schools, conceding that such things have nothing to do with increasing educational achievement or with stimulating the productive ethos, is that since people spend so considerable a percentage of their lifetime at school, why not make their stay at school as pleasant as possible?

It was quite a season for the educators. Head Start programs for the particularly disadvantaged? Of course —only they didn't work. Compensatory education for those who had slighted particular educational disciplines? Of course—only they didn't work. A higher ratio

of teachers to students in order to provide more individual attention? Of course—only it didn't work. Compulsory integration in order to raise the standard of achievement for the minority students? Of course—only that
didn't work. Local control of a school would bring parent
participation and student enthusiasm? It didn't work out
that way. Compulsory integration of students so as to
increase interracial harmony and understanding? Of
course—only, of course, that didn't work.

The true crisis, really, is a crisis of faith more than
anything else, faith in the thaumaturgic properties of
Education. The social crisis brought on by the busing of
students to remote schools for the purpose of racial balance was by contrast a real and immediate thing, reaching its peak in 1972 when George Wallace won the
Democratic nomination in Michigan. The deflation of
liberal educational dogma wasn't the kind of thing that
brings on instant public reaction. Some of the programs
designed to administer compensatory education are
being phased out. Here and there the taxpayers voted
down demands of fresh capital for education. But this
after all was inevitable, considering the graph. If it had
continued at the inclination of the fifties and sixties, as
with welfare, there would not have been public money
left to pay the street-sweepers by 1980. The teachers, in
whose pockets (it is estimated) 68 percent of all fresh
appropriations came to rest, are dug in against retrench-
ment. Occasionally one comes across a faint Nockean
blip from an academic quarter: too many people are
going to college, it is here and there discreetly whispered.
Professor Ernest van den Haag has circulated the figures:
whereas it is estimated that only those with an IQ of 110
or higher can absorb a college education, and only 25
percent of the people have that IQ, 43 percent of

college-age Americans are matriculating in college. Never mind, the colleges would gradually change in character—as Nock predicted they would do. They would continue to confer college degrees by the simple expedient of reducing the requirements for earning them; and, as Christopher Jencks suggested of the secondary schools, they would continue to exercise the function of providing pleasant surroundings for a significant period of one's lifetime. Van den Haag's warning that we are graduating a class of people in whom we are cultivating discontent and frustration is unheeded—in part because the danger is so far unrealized. Perhaps in due course we shall face a lumpenbaccalaureate class that disdains the jobs for which its members consider themselves unfit, in virtue of the exalted testimonials to their achievements as rendered in their diplomas. But that is in the future. Meanwhile the governments, federal, state, and local, continue to feed the system, within which, we happily assume, the genuinely gifted are taking furtive nourishment, and the educational bureaucracy is content, not to say fat. The crisis is a theorists' crisis, more keenly than a public crisis.

By contrast, the crisis of the private schools, primarily the religious schools—primarily the Catholic schools—is immediate. The parochial schools are closing at the rate of two per day. The President of the United States and other doomsayers keep warning the public about the high cost of permitting this attrition. By the end of the decade, the President warned in the spring of 1972, if the private schools continue to close at the current rate, the public will need to spend $4 billion more per year in order to provide schooling for the Catholic population and, besides that, will need to finance $5 billion for extra buildings. But The Public is, let's face it, unfrightened by the prospect of spending another $4 billion per year, eight years from now, on anything.

The pressures on the private schools are enormous, but not so the pressures on the nation, notwithstanding that even the Supreme Court goes along with the economic argument. Every time the Court disallows a private school relief measure, in every single case designed by public officials who are implausibly charged with surreptitious ambitions to establishmentarianize, spokesmen for the Court first pay tribute to the economic sacrifices of the constituents of the private schools; and then say "No." As a matter of fact it was the Supreme Court itself that held, long ago in 1925 (*Pierce v. Society of Sisters*), that the state of Oregon had no right to require attendance at a public school. "The fundamental theory of liberty upon which all governments in this Union repose excludes any general power of the State to standardize its children by forcing them to accept instruction from public teachers only. The child is not the mere creature of the State. . . ." And in 1952 (*Zorach*), retreating slightly from the hard-line position against released time for religious instruction, taken in *McCollum*, the Court, via Justice Douglas, took time out to be positively evangelical. "We are a religious people whose institutions presuppose a Supreme Being. . . . When the State encourages religious instruction or cooperates with religious authorities by adjusting the schedule of public events to sectarian needs, it follows the best of our traditions. For then it respects the religious nature of our people and accommodates the public service to their spiritual needs. To hold that it may not would be to find in the Constitution a requirement that the government show a callous indifference to religious groups. That would be preferring those who believe in no religion over those who believe." Perhaps Mr. Douglas had in mind the language of the

Northwest Ordinance, which provided that, "Religion, morality and knowledge being necessary to good government and the happiness of mankind, schools and the means of education shall forever be encouraged."

And then, when in 1971 it began (*Lemon*) the series of recent decisions that would result in plainly forbidding *any* arrangement, however circumspect, however removed from any effort to "establish" religion in any communicable sense of the word, the Court paid lavish social tribute to its victim. "Finally, nothing we have said can be construed to disparage the role of the church-related elementary and secondary schools in our national life. Their contribution has been and is enormous. Nor do we ignore their economic plight in a period of rising costs and expanding need. Taxpayers have been spared vast sums by the maintenance of these educational institutions by religious organizations, largely by the gifts of faithful adherents. . . ." However . . .

Castigo te non quod odio habeam, sed quod amem.

It was widely assumed for a few tense years after *Lemon*, and before *Committee for Public Education* (June, 1973), that a formula had finally been discovered. The thinking was as follows. Once a dollar is taken from a citizen, it becomes a public dollar, and cannot be used in any way to support a religious institution, never mind for the moment that under the GI Bill of Rights you could use your government grant to pay tuition at any accredited school anywhere. However (so the argument goes), until that dollar is taken from the citizen, it is his. Why can't the government permit a tax credit to the citizen who spends his own money on a socially desirable activity, whatever its sectarian ties: non-public schools, for instance, even if they are Lutheran or Catholic in affiliation? The Court teased these thinkers along when, in 1970 (*Walz*), it wrote so encouragingly, "The grant of a tax exemption is not sponsorship since the government does not transfer part of its revenue to churches but simply abstains from demanding that the church support the state." But when the great decision of June, 1973, came in, notwithstanding that a dissenter leaned heavily on the passage quoted above, the decision of the Court was, once again, "No." There appeared to be no further lines of retreat, no prospect for a solution.

It is worth noting at this point that although the old sectarian animosities linger, they are not endemic, not what they used to be, though they are no less virulent in some of those who are affected, mostly members of the older generations. The anti-Catholicism of the Paul Blanshard School, for instance, is significantly diluted. It is pleasant to conclude that the Sons of Blanshard grew in toleration. It is more exact to say that Romanism yielded to the Zeitgeist, and that the features of Catholicism that most prominently antagonized non-Catholic Americans are almost lost in the homogenization of the national religious profile. Even the attention-drawing abstention from eating meat on Fridays is gone as irritant-symbol. The authority of the Pope is less conspicuously questioned by Protestant than by Catholic theologians. The old, abrasive doctrine of the One True Church is unbreathed from the pulpit. Papal pronouncements on birth control, the sundering social-religious issue of the 1960's, are simply unheeded, except by the few, and it is serenely expected that a new Pope will recast the pronouncements of his predecessor so as to fit them into a cozy paradigmatic grotto before which one worships, or wonders, but never, among the unsaintly, repines. It is not for us to say whether the solution to the population problem on earth will relieve the population problem in paradise. Meanwhile attendance at Mass, in most churches, requires the fiercest concentration in order to escape involvement in the punishment of the liturgy the modernists have prepared for those who love them not. The evolution of the Latin Mass can be compared to the neighborhood school. At first it was ruled merely that the vernacular Mass should not be proscribed. Now the Latin Mass, like the uni-racial neighborhood school, wakes up to find itself proscribed, and those who seek it out are a frustrate class.

The economic plight of the Catholic parochial schools, which are 60 percent of the nation's private schools, is most generally ascribed to the increased cost in teacher salaries required by the swelling percentage of faculty hired from the ranks of laymen. It is seldom pondered why this should be so, why there is so sharp a decline in membership in the religious orders. Nor is the subject generally raised why, with the increase in the general affluence, it should nevertheless be harder to raise money for religious education now than fifty years ago. Visible from where I live is a peninsula with its huge and luxurious mansion and auxiliary houses acquired from an estate by a teaching order of nuns during the Great Depression and transformed into a girls' boarding school. In a very few years it had greatly succeeded, achieving academic excellence and social distinction, and during the 1950's there were several applicants for every matriculant. Two years ago it closed its doors, leaving the eastern seaboard without a single academically distinguished boarding school for Catholic girls. That school was not closed by the Supreme Court, nor by the indigence of its patrons.

All of which is by way of saying that the problems of the religious schools are not caused only by the Supreme Court. Conceivably, at the present rate of indifference, the private religious schools would wither and die from lack of patronage even if they were fully subsidized by the state. So much for full disclosure.

The present contention, however, is over the reach of the Establishment of Religion Clause, and the very weaknesses of the sectarian schools are a sociological datum underscoring the point that this is the silliest of historical seasons to invoke the First Amendment as an excuse for standing in the way of Establishment. It is not plausibly argued that any American religion is nowadays seeking stealthily to gain advantage over other religions by conscripting the machinery of government to its peculiar advantage, and in the light of these coordinates, the tortuous reasoning of the Supreme Court decision (*"As the parties here must concede, tax reductions authorized by this law flow primarily to the parents of children attending sectarian, nonpublic schools. Without intimating whether this factor alone might have controlling significance in another context in some future case, it should be apparent that in terms of the potential divisiveness of any legislative measure the narrowness of the benefited class would be an important factor. . . ."—Committee for Public Education,* 1973) strikes the mind as sheer surrealism, the kind of eristic patter more appropriate to the Fellows of All Souls diverting themselves over their port than to Supreme Court Justices concerting to tell blue-collar parents that the Constitution won't let them, in effect, send their children to the parochial school.

It can of course be argued (and away from the public view it often is) that if the victimized minority—mostly Catholics, but also a few Protestants and Jews—cannot muster the political heft to assert themselves, they cannot expect relief. The point, however cynical, is well made historically, but it is morally smug: the Negro minority was for many years not without just claims, but without political leverage.

One must ask: (1) Should not the just claims of the

dispirited occupy our attention? (2) Aren't we (see below) in fact easing the Supreme Court over into a position of authority unrelated to its Constitutional purpose and inimical to republican institutions? And, finally, (3) Isn't the whole of the country likely to suffer extra-economic privations from the closing down of these schools? In fact the religious-oriented schools are the great bulk of the surviving private schools. Perhaps in due course we shall move into a voucher system in which the community will pay the basic tuition cost at any grade school the student patronizes, even as the GI Bill permits the veteran to select his own college. Pending that day, the immediate concern is to husband such private schools as there are, wherein, less hampered by general regulations, there is more opportunity to experiment, to cultivate excellence and diversity, to provide safe and reasonable means for exercising the inclinations, academic, social, and spiritual, of such people as are dissatisfied either with public schools in general, or with such public schools as now they are assigned to by the complex interaction of social, political, and judicial pressures flowing through their school boards.

The following should be adopted as an Amendment to the Constitution.

No child shall be denied admission to a public school, by the United States or by any State, on account of race, creed, color, or national origin, notwithstanding any provision in the Constitution of the United States or of any State. Nor shall any relief authorized by any legislature for children attending nonpublic schools be denied by virtue of any provision in the Constitution of the United States or of any State.

The proposed amendment is framed with attention to legal and Constitutional niceties. It is easier to prohibit than to enjoin (indeed, the Bill of Rights is mostly a catalogue of prohibitions, like the old doges' inaugural oaths). It was not contemplated that the illegalization of compulsory segregation should lead to the illegalization of uni-racial schools if these merely reflected the incidence of residential racial patterns. The Court's suspicion of Southern motives, altogether justified in many instances, caused it to upset successive Southern arrangements on the grounds that residually uni-racial schools suggested nothing more than successful subterfuge. The Supreme Court (at this writing) has never upset schools that are preponderantly of one race in areas that have no history of compulsory segregation. But lower federal courts began doing so, and it was this that precipitated the crisis of 1972, to some extent stilled by Congress's injunction (at Mr. Nixon's request) to the courts to desist from further rulings until a) the Supreme Court had resolved unreconciled rulings of the lower courts, and b) Congress had considered the Court's ruling, perhaps availing itself of such rights as it may have, under the Fourteenth Amendment, to specify the means of putting it into effect.

In the event that the Court should rule that it has direct responsibility under the Fourteenth Amendment, it is stopped by the phrase "notwithstanding any provision in the Constitution of the United States or [and this for the benefit of the runaway states, of which there are usually one or two] of any State." One is left with effective legislation freezing the role of the courts safely past the point taken at *Brown v. Board of Education*, but short of the biracializing compulsions of the judges whose decisions in Richmond, Charlotte, and Detroit triggered the convulsion of 1972.

The arguments against as well as for compulsory integration are well enough known. The emphasis here is, as ever, procedural. The decision which school to send a student to (where there are alternatives) is a fine balance of considerations which parents in different circumstances will weigh differently. Today's emphasis is gone tomorrow, and tomorrow's the day after. During the fifties the cry was for integrated schools. Even midway into the sixties, the call by black members of the community was not for repealing integration, but for withdrawing from it that priority of consideration that had been assigned to it. Some members of the black community went far in the other direction, towards separatism, and there are traces still in the colleges of sullen enclaves protesting what they see as an ignominious assumption that racial mixture brings them what racial purity cannot. White families are not opposed to busing under certain circumstances—to reach, let us say, an outstanding school, or to take a gifted child to a remote music teacher. On the whole, though, the preference is for the neighborhood school. And on the whole the neighborhood school, particularly in the North, is preponderantly of the same color. But those who, reasoning from their attachment to their own community, pronounce invidiously on adjacent communities are no doubt reprehensible insofar as they flatter parochial prejudices into a kind of cultural and even biological ethnocentrism. But it is to defy the analysis that brought us to consider especially the plight of the American Negro to say that he has reached overnight a parity with those who were called upon to respond to appeals from an organization calmly designated as the National Association for the Advancement of Colored People. Advancement into parity. The means of effecting that advancement continue to be the subject of considerable thought and experimentation, but it is no longer accepted as axiomatic that integrated classrooms, effected if necessary by busing whites or blacks over considerable distances, is the way. And, at the theoretical level, much much thought has been given to the question: Where, where on earth, in the Constitution, or in the nebulae that formed it, is the warrant for punishing the prejudice of an adult by sending his child to a school far away? Only a tiny number of white people (4 percent) want busing, and not many more (9 percent) Negroes. The proposed amendment reaffirms the proscription against the denial of a right, but lays to rest, forever, the strangely conceived right of the courts to prescribe exactly the racial divisions in geographical districts.

There has probably never been a period in academic history in which there has been greater bewilderment over how, exactly, to improve the quality of general education, the degree of literacy. Deweyite optimism, one notes, is undermined. The easy notion that true literacy proceeds exponentially is shattered as we reflect on the quality of the public debates between Lincoln and Douglas when 40 percent of the American people were illiterate, and the debates between Nixon and Kennedy, when 2 percent of the American people were illiterate. This essay does not seek to suggest substantive means of improving either pedagogical techniques or educational goals; merely, once again, some means of freeing up the system, so that new techniques can be tried, and old—and new—values invigorated.

The key, as with the private schools, is surely: noncoercive education. Once again, procedure. The loosening of the molds they are always building.

And the second half of the amendment is pure clarification. It lets stand the First Amendment in the meaning it had for almost one hundred and seventy-five years. There is to be no establishment of religion, no prohibition against the free exercise thereof. But the Establishment clause is not to be taken to mean what the Court has recently taken it to mean, against reason, history, and the desire of most citizens.

Most of the arguments against resorting to amendments to the Constitution are sound, and the best reason for a presumptive opposition to amendments is the rhetoric with which their endorsement is so often accompanied, the seizures of plebiscitary indignation. But when the presumption against amending the Constitution evolves into a categorical opposition, one has bumped up against a mystique, an examination of which, in the American example, tells us a great deal about our developing relationship with the Constitution or, more exactly, with the Supreme Court.

Here, I think, are the principal points to make. The Constitution—in particular certain phrases in it, some in the body of the Constitution, others in the amendments to it—is understood differently by different persons, and this is so even among people of comparable academic background and devotion to the ideals of the Founders. Examples abound, and there are interesting theological parallels. Justice Hugo Black used to say that he understood the phrase in the First Amendment that Congress shall make no law "abridging the freedom of speech" as all, really, that he needed to know in order to side against *any* law abridging the freedom of speech, including libel legislation. In the language of religion, this would be called fundamentalism, the kind of thing Clarence Darrow amused himself with, at the expense of William Jennings Bryan, at the great Scopes trial when he asked Bryan such questions as how had the snakes ambulated before they were made by the Lord to use their bellies, and how exactly had Jonah accommodated to the inside of a whale.

In handling myths to live by, the exegete can be indispensable, and it is partly in recognition of this that the Roman Catholic religion has its own Supreme Court—the "Church," empowered, like the U.S. Supreme Court, to decide which are the doctrinally tolerable, which the intolerable, understandings of Biblical assertion or adumbration: where one must deal with Jonah-in-the-whale with the kind of literal attachment that Justice Black devoted to the free speech clause in the First Amendment. The Catholic Church deals of course in another plane of human allegiance. The Constitution, we have been brought up to believe, is what the Supreme Court says it is; and indeed it is, if necessary at bayonet point. In the current season, Catholic doctrine is only formally what the Pope says it is. The survival—at least in this world—of Catholics who dissent from some of the doctrinal directions of the Pope exemplifies the difference between spiritual and temporal authority. An American who believes that the Supreme Court has erred in interpreting the Constitution has no alternative but to comply with the Court's interpretation, however ardently he chooses to inveigh against it. The Catholic, in the modern age, is immune from any temporal sanction of the Church. Nor is the Church organized to detect discreet noncompliance. It can only impose public punishment on those who profess their heresies.

The underappreciated point about the Supreme Court is that it has become a kind of moral-secular authority. Adult men and women, staring hard at a clause in the Constitution of the United States that forbids an establishment of religion and recognizing no reasonable nexus between that prohibition and the recital, at their local public school, of a public prayer, jointly formulated by rabbis, ministers, and priests, receive on Monday what might be called a juridical bull from the Supreme Court, and on Tuesday there is compliance. Their docility is, in the religious sense, exemplary. *If that is what the Supreme Court says*, the most urbane American lawyers, governors, ministers, and journalists will say—*why that is how it shall be*. It is my point that it is something more than compliance that then results. It is something more akin to what, in religion, they call "internal assent." If-that-is-what-the-Supreme-Court-says-that-is-the-way-it-will-be, graduates towards: If that is what the Supreme Court says, that is the way it *ought* to be. The docility becomes religious in character.

The objection that, after all, we have had a number of Constitutional amendments in recent years does not affect the insight. Because the amendments, with an insignificant but nonetheless interesting exception, have merely codified popular passions, some of them consolidated (no poll tax), others impulsive and manipulated (no booze). But (save for the, largely irrelevant, exception) there has been no Constitutional amendment the purpose of which was to revise the interpretations of a Supreme Court, notwithstanding egregious provocations by the Court, most recently during the fifties and sixties, when it became a commonplace to refer to the "Warren Revolution." Those who hoped for the status quo ante— in the area of legislative representation, criminal procedure, or freedom of association—spoke big, and filed their proposed Constitutional reforms; but, in fact, it was a ritual. They were really waiting for a few popes to die, knowing that only fresh popes could authoritatively change doctrines that were fast being accepted or—received.

Towards the end of the nineteenth century Congress discovered the joys of the income tax, but in 1895 the

Court (*Pollock v. Farmers' Loan & Trust Company*) ruled that the law was unconstitutional, that it treated income from property as indirect income taxable by Congress, whereas it was in reality direct income taxable only through the states. It is significant that eighteen years went by before *Pollock* was overturned. And during those eighteen years, a series of Supreme Court decisions had modified the Court's opposition to the income tax, so much so that it was questioned by some whether the Sixteenth Amendment was really necessary.

Two points: the first, agencies of government tend to concert so as to overcome any obstacle that stands between them and the acquisition of a taxpayer's dollar (I note in the following chapter that the protections of the Fifth Amendment are abruptly excused when it comes to dealing with Internal Revenue). The second: as a matter of historical fact, the Supreme Court was itself in rapid retreat from its own decision, and accordingly opposition to the Sixteenth Amendment (there was some, it was vigorous, and it was substantially rejected as hysterical because opponents of the tax were going to such preposterous lengths as to warn that in due course the income tax might rise as high as 10 percent) did not rely heavily on the authority of the *Pollock* decision which was wasting away by attrition. Even then, it required four years to put together the necessary three-fourths majority to override.

Since then there have been several other amendments. Briefly noted, the reconstitution of the Senate, a populist demand, was not an issue that touched the Court, there being no middle ground between the traditional arrangement and the proposed new arrangement such as would invite the Court's intervention. (It is interesting, in the light of subsequent Court inverventions on the side of one-man one-vote, that there are only two provisions in the Constitution that were stipulated by the Founders as removed from the amendment process. One, and only for a brief period, protected the slave clauses; the other guaranteed (Article 5) that for the lifetime of the Constitution, no state, without its consent, would be deprived of its equal vote in the Senate.)

Prohibition, promulgated in 1919 (Amendment 18) and terminated in 1933 (Amendment 21), was in no way a reaction, in or out, to Court decisions. In 1920 (Amendment 19) the vote for women was ratified; there was of course no sense in which this was done athwart any ruling, or sentiment, of the Court. The Twentieth, Twenty-second, Twenty-third, and Twenty-fifth Amendments (1933, 1951, 1961, 1967) were purely administrative in character, rescheduling Presidential inaugurations, limiting the President to two terms in office, giving to the District of Columbia an electoral vote in Presidential elections, and specifying procedure in the event of Presidential disability. There had been no record of any commitment by the Court on any of the points.

In 1964 (Amendment 24) the poll tax was abolished. Here indeed there had been pressure by the Court. But it was congruent pressure. The Court had been asked to entertain, and indeed had (*Breedlove*, 1937) encouraged, the notion that poll taxes might be an unconstitutional impediment to a voter's access to the polls as guaranteed under the post-Civil War Amendments. The Twenty-sixth Amendment (1971) was the nearest thing to a Constitutional stampede in American history, passing through the legislatures in three months, in contrast with the previous record-maker, the repeal of Prohibition. One assumes that the relative leisure (nine months) with which the state legislatures handled repeal was either a cavalier demonstration of national continence, or testimony to the redundancy of legislation that licenses the breathing of air. By contrast the panicked vote to enfranchise the eighteen-year-olds suggested that many legislators sensed the alternative might be a juvenocracy brought in by force. The Court had never committed itself, in any discernible way, in favor of the twenty-one-year-old tradition.

The proposed twenty-seventh Amendment (women's rights) flits about among the state legislatures making uneven progress. It is held by its sponsors to be not only harmonious with the Constitution, but a blossom of it, by the Nineteenth Amendment, and there is certainly no inflection in any Supreme Court decision that might be summoned as in opposition to this Amendment.

I am suggesting what must by now be obvious. The public—under the tutelage of its moral and intellectual leaders—is being trained, as regards the Supreme Court of the United States when it is interpreting the Constitution, to accept its rulings as if rendered ex cathedra, on questions of faith and morals. Thus candidates for political office are routinely quoted as saying that they disapprove (let us say) of busing, but that if the Supreme Court rules otherwise, that of course will be that. It is a far different statement from one, republican in analysis and spirit, which would read, "I am against busing, but if the Supreme Court rules otherwise, I shall abide by its decision—pending the final verdict on the question by the people through the amendment process." The durability of the United States Constitution is in part testimony to the genius of its architects. But it endures also because it changes. It changes in considerable part at the shaping of the Supreme Court, concerning whose elaborations of the Constitution much poetry has been written, mostly by those who, at any particular historical period, are enthusiastic about the direction the Court is taking. The public needs to experience a release from a subtle thralldom to judicial morality. The polls are clear on the matter known as busing: the people are overwhelmingly opposed. They are clear that the voters are also opposed (though by a slightly lesser margin) to the total secularization of the schools. A constitutional amendment, done athwart the will of the Court for the first time in modern history, would accomplish more than simply bringing relief to the majority who consider themselves victims of judicial usurpation. It would deliver the Republic from a presumptuous ethical-political tribunal which has come to treat the Constitution with something like an author's possessiveness. Thus is mocked their fellow Americans' powers of thought analysis, and their august commitment to self-rule. Accordingly, the special need for a constitutional amendment.

CHAPTER IV

Crime

Towards Speedier Justice

ON September 6, 1901, President McKinley was assassinated. On October 29, 1901, seven weeks later, Leon Czolgosz, the assassin, was executed. The allegation has never been made, or if so it has not reached this cloister, that Mr. Czolgosz was unfairly tried, though as a matter of fact, applying contemporary criteria, he was most unfairly tried. On June 5, 1968, Robert Kennedy was assassinated. Forty-five weeks later, after a fourteen-week trial, Sirhan Sirhan was found guilty. As a matter of fact he was sentenced to death and is, of course, five years later, alive (one wonders if Lloyds of London gives specially reduced life insurance rates for Americans sentenced to death). For those who reason from these historical antipodes that the judicial process in the United States is greatly refined by the passage of time I adduce a comparison. In June of 1971 the New York *Times* began publication of the so-called Pentagon Papers. The Justice Department protested, and the federal district court took two days to decline to hand down an injunction forbidding the New York *Times* from continuing the series. The Justice Department appealed. The court of appeals took two days to reverse the lower court.

The *Times* in turn appealed to the Supreme Court. Six days later that Court overruled the court of appeals, authorizing the resumption of the publication of the Papers.

Several advocates of the *Times'* position furiously deplored the slowness of the Supreme Court in handing down its judgment. Chief Justice Burger, dissenting, took thought to do a little deploring of his own. He commented that it takes a certain amount of time to read through the 7,000 pages necessary in order to weigh the arguments of the government that the national security justified prior restraint; and he pointed out that the New York *Times'* editorial board had deliberated no less than three and a half months between receiving the Papers and beginning to serialize them, a hiatus that suggested that the editors of the *Times* thought it important to go over the material with some care, and were prepared to withhold them from the public for several months. Under the circumstances it hardly seemed inordinate for the Supreme Court of the United States to take six days to review the same material.

The wonder is that the courts—three courts—should have acted so fast. The episode is by way of background, to remind oneself that encephalitis is not hopelessly advanced in judicial America, that there was a recorded remission as recently as in 1971 in response to great pressure. Not exactly public pressure—the people of the United States had not risen, demanding to know there and then and without further delay exactly what Secretary Rusk had said to Secretary McNamara in 1961 about the disposition of the Seventh Fleet. It was the pressure of the foremost newspaper in the United States and the civil rights lobby that succeeded in getting all three divisions of the federal judiciary to transact in a fortnight a controversy of far-reaching Constitutional implications, more complicated even than the vexed question, Was it Sirhan Sirhan who killed Robert Kennedy, or were the two hundred witnesses who saw him do it in a hypnotic trance?

Shortly after the event, in the summer of 1971, the government moved against the man who in apparent violation of the law had turned the Pentagon Papers over to the New York *Times*. Thirteen months after the *Times* had begun publishing the Papers, the trial of Daniel Ellsberg began. The defense was outraged that the judge exercised his rights, under federal procedure, to dominate the jury selection. Even then it took ten days. If the defense had had its way, no doubt as in the trial of Bobby Seale in New Haven, Connecticut, jury selection would have taken three months. The defense then raised an objection on a technical point. The judge said no. The appellate court said no. Justice William Douglas of the Supreme Court said yes, and halted the trial. In late July the government petitioned the whole of the Supreme Court to meet and overrule Justice Douglas, but the Court declined to act (Summer-time/An' the livin' is eas-y) so the interlocutory decree of Justice Douglas passed over into the routine calendar. In due course Justice Douglas was overruled, and the trial resumed. The defense filed other motions. It was argued, among other things, that the jurors, experiencing such tiresome delays, must necessarily have developed an animosity against a defendant whose legal motions had so severely ravaged their schedules, and under the circumstances the trial should begin afresh, with a brand-new jury. Judge Byrne disagreed. But a higher court admonished him to get a fresh jury. He acquiesced. A new trial began on January 17. On May 11, sixteen weeks after the reconvened trial, Ellsberg having at that point spent nearly one million dollars in lawyer's fees and expenses, the judge dismissed all charges. The dismissal had nothing to do with interpreting the Constitution, or administering the law, or vindicating Ellsberg. It had to do with protesting the felonious improprieties of two convicted Watergaters who had burglarized the office of Ellsberg's psychiatrist—uncovering nothing about Ellsberg as it happened. About just such a situation was the observation made by a puzzled observer of American judicial practice, "Only a system with limitless patience with irrationality could tolerate the fact that where there has been one wrong, the defendant's, he will be punished, but where there have been two wrongs—the defendant's and the [police] officer's—both will go free."

Justice McNally, retiring recently as appellate judge in New York, observed that it takes *nine to ten times* as long to try a case as it did when he first practiced as a judge twenty-seven years earlier. In the year 1900, the population of the borough of Manhattan was 1,900,000, and there were on hand, to take care of malefactors, six felony judges. Today the population of the borough is reduced to 1,500,000 and there are thirty felony judges, and they are behind in their work. In the District of Columbia Court of General Sessions there were 1,500 defendants awaiting trial in July, 1969. In the United States District Court, 1,700 defendants were awaiting trial. The average time between indictment and the disposition of a case in the district court is two hundred and fifty-four days. It is twice that in the Court of General Sessions. If you add on the time for an appeal, then the average span of a criminal proceeding comes to just under two years.

Meanwhile, in most categories, crime has greatly risen. Though murder is down from the high-water mark of the mid-thirties, half again as many Americans (8,000) were killed intentionally in the United States in 1969 as in

Vietnam. Burglary, rape, mugging, are all up, at three to five times the increase in population. The police commissioner of New York recently drew attention to some illuminating figures. In 1960, the police in New York City made 36,000 felony arrests. In 1970, they made 94,000 felony arrests. Of these, 522 went to trial, or less than one percent. "The rest of them were, quotes, disposed of. Disposed of means dismissed outright, reduced to misdemeanors via plea bargaining, [or] reduced to much lesser felonies via plea bargaining."

The length of time required to try a case, the long delays, the rising crime figures, the reduction in the gravity of charges, the diminishing number of convictions, require that one identify—once again—the procedural problems. It would all be easier if one could know how many innocent men were convicted, say thirty years ago, as a consequence of the failure of the Supreme Court adequately to elaborate the rights of the defendant, a large enterprise of the Warren Court during the fifties and sixties (*Mallory, Mapp, Gideon, Escobedo, Massiah, Miranda*). Not that a society is bound to endorse any measure the effect of which is to diminish the number of innocents convicted. If this were the only imperative, it could of course be achieved by the simple act of ceasing to prosecute anyone. As it is, we do not know even how to plot a graph suggesting how we are doing in reconciling our various concerns. It is known only that the ratio of convictions to crimes committed continues to decrease; that the length of time required to prosecute has become inordinate (one despairing judge put it that "it has become ridiculously hard to prove simple guilt"). Turning the murder of Robert Kennedy into a whodunnit is testimony to the total ascendancy of ritual in American jurisprudence.

And correlatively, the cost of an exhaustive defense has become surrealistic (a young but highly experienced lawyer with the firm of Edward Bennett Williams has remarked that if he were himself prosecuted for a serious crime, he could not afford to hire a lawyer to pursue all the avenues he knew were available to him): and the burdens mount on the court-appointed lawyers.

There are votaries of the Bill of Rights who worship with theological passion, transmuting every phrase into full-blown dogma. It is this compulsion, resulting in an overelaboration of the rights of the defendant, that has caused the Bill of Rights to serve so perversely the interests of lawbreakers. One sometimes wonders what the American Civil Liberties Union would have done if the Bill of Rights had included the article, "Congress shall pass no law obstructing the pursuit of justice."

It has become a commonplace, but is worth stressing here, that the extension of any single right to infinite length almost necessarily gets in the way of other rights, infinitely extended. Professor Sidney Hook wrote a fine book, *The Paradoxes of Freedom*, on the subject. How does one achieve, simultaneously, a totally free press, and a totally fair trial? How can one absolutize the Fifth Amendment's guarantee against self-incrimination, and the Sixth Amendment's guarantee of the right to compel testimony? It is the job of the judiciary, building on the law, to reconcile rights, rather than to draw any single right out to lengths so extreme as to unbalance the structure. Unbalancing the structure is here defined as forgetting the purpose of the adversary process. It is designed, with subtle qualifications not relevant here, to arrive at the truth; to determine whether a defendant is in fact guilty or not guilty of committing a particular crime. Judge Laurence Wren, who presided over the second trial of the notorious Miranda for rape, reminisced after Miranda took the witness stand and admitted that he had raped the girl (the jury having been sent out): "When the verdict was finally in, I suddenly realized, with complete amazement and disgust, that we had not dealt at all during the nine-day trial with the basic question of guilt or innocence."

The adversary process invites abuse, and there has developed among professionals who participate in the process a highly elastic ethic concerning the abuses of it. If in an adversary proceeding the defense can get away with taking such advantages as it takes, it is expected to take such advantages. Justice Robert Jackson in 1949 (*Watts v. Indiana*) observed matter-of-factly that "any lawyer worth his salt will tell the suspect in no uncertain terms to make no statements to police under any circumstances." This, curiously, becomes an ethic of sorts—resisted, but without great effect, by such as a former Attorney General. Mr. Nicholas Katzenbach, for instance, has written, "I have never understood why the gangster should be made the model and all others raised, in the name of equality, to his level of success in suppressing evidence. This is simply the proposition that if some can beat the rap, all must beat the rap." A demonstration that rich felons go unhung is not an argument for freeing poor felons, but for redoubling efforts against rich felons. In 1966, the Supreme Court ruled (*Miranda*) that no defendant who had given evidence against himself need submit at a trial to the use of that evidence unless he had "knowingly and intelligently" waived a lawyer. (Subsequent practice suggests that the court is satisfied that a lawyer is "intelligently" waived if the suspect is informed that, a) anything he says can be used against him, b) he need not answer any question, c) he is entitled to a lawyer, and d) if he doesn't have the money for a lawyer, the state will furnish one.)

If Mr. Jackson is right, no one will "intelligently" waive a lawyer unless he simply desires to confess, in which case the adversary proceeding, for the purposes of this discussion, or any other, is suspended. No lawyer, if Jackson is right, will suffer his client to confess, except presumably as part of a bargain.

One sees that the adversary process proceeds as a kind of game, with each side attempting to maximize its advantages. The opinions handed down by the Warren Court are widely held responsible for the disequilibrium.

Granted the adversary process has always had something of the structure of a game. John Stuart Mill alluded to it. "[People] speak and act as if they regarded a criminal trial as a sort of game, partly of chance, partly of skill, in which the proper end to be aimed at is not that the truth may be discovered, but that both parties may have fair play; in a word, that whether a guilty person should be acquitted or punished, may be, as near as possible, an even chance." To be sure, law-as-a-game continues to be intellectually resisted. Professor James Vorenberg of the Harvard Law School accosts the problem directly. "Criminal justice is not a sport or game, and notions of fairness derived from the moral structure of games, premised on legitimation of self-interests to the fullest extent consistent with the game, are by no means persuasive." Such arguments may not be persuasive, but they have most certainly persuaded: that is the way the system is working.

A proposed reform:
The Fifth Amendment (as currently interpreted) should be repealed.
Procedures should adapt to the criterion: Did he do it?
Procedures should adapt to the goal of speedier justice.

❧

It is worth pausing here to inspect the philosophical implications. The libertarian's presumptive sympathies lie quite rightly with the individual when the state itself is engaging him. The libertarian is prescriptively committed to the doctrine that by the historical evidence and by the nature of the political dynamic, the state tends (in John Adams' phrase) to turn every contingency into an excuse for aggrandizing power within itself. There is little doubt—to take a recent example—that the men who surrounded Richard Nixon seized upon security leaks, considering which their concern was wholly legitimate, as a contingency that authorized the government to assault the privacy, and undermine the rights, of target individuals. John Dean was the phraseologist of the enterprise, and in giving us "maximize the incumbency," he did as well as Orwell could have done. Fortunately most of the plans were conceptualized, rather than realized; but only, it would seem, for reasons of funk, rather than scruple.

But there is a difference between the state when it is acting as agent for its own aggrandizement, and the state when it is acting in behalf of an aggrieved citizen. *The State of California v. Sirhan Sirhan* is viewed only by the undiscriminating as merely another production of The State vs. The Individual. It is closer to the truth to personalize the contest as The Widow Kennedy vs. Sirhan Sirhan. Or, at the highest generic level, The Wives and Children of America vs. Sirhan Sirhan. The state's initiative on behalf of the widow Kennedy is the discharge of a primal responsibility, by the state on behalf of a citizen. To disparage the state by the use of libertarian rhetoric in such encounters as these is to undermine not the presumptions of Big Brother, but warranties to the individual who, as victim or as the victim's next of kin, looks to the government precisely to vindicate its corollary responsibility, having failed in its first responsibility. The first is to guard life and property. The corollary is to prosecute those transgressors upon life and property whom it has failed to protect the victim against. There is no plausible excuse for the state except to defend the individual. The individual having been violated, the state asserts the claims of the individual, dead, maimed, or deprived. Obviously the claims of the innocent, mistaken for the transgressor, are as great as those of the victim, whence the adversary process. But the rhetoric of civil liberties during the past decade has concerned itself almost exclusively over the claims of the former, in disregard of the claims of the latter, and that is perversion.

Miranda, as noted, held not only that the accused must "intelligently" waive a lawyer. It also held that he must be informed in clear and unequivocal language that he has the right to remain silent; that anything he says can be used in court against him; that if he should at any point indicate a desire to remain silent, interrogation should thereupon terminate; and that if the accused should proceed to talk in such a way as to aid the prosecution, the burden devolved on the government to prove that the defendant knowingly and intelligently waived his privilege against self-incrimination and counsel. Any statement by the accused elicited without regard to these rules cannot be admitted into evidence; nor may it be introduced as evidence that the defendant, when questioned, stood mute, or even that he invoked his privilege in the face of the accusation. That decision discouraged spontaneous confessions but, alongside other decisions (principally *Mapp*), also had the effect of removing from the courtroom incriminating evidence the existence of which was divulged by the accused under unlicensed circumstances. The effect has been to exclude the most useful evidence of all—the defendant's own statements, with respect to which the jury can most responsibly weigh the question of guilt or innocence.

The recent convention that evidence must be excluded because it was obtained by unlicensed means is not reasonable. Its sole justification is to punish the policeman or the prosecutor for having stolen a base, to use a metaphor appropriate to the game-view of the adversary process. But this is an abstractionists' penalty, childishly reliant on superficial logical relations. However zestful the constable, to rob him of a conviction is not to punish him, in the sense that he would experience punishment if he were fined, jailed, or demoted. Free the defendant by denying to the jury knowledge of the incriminating evidence, and you deprive the constable of the platonic satisfaction he'd have taken from a conviction. But his punishment is more nearly like the athlete's whom the referee rules against as having been offside. Some of the most valuable players have the heaviest dockets of violations. They are seldom penalized by those who count—the coach, the owners, the public. They get away with it often enough to keep them doing it. The police, viewed as players, do not suffer from the disallowance of evidence improperly obtained. That the defense gains does not mean that the prosecution suffers, except as we permit ourselves to accept the subversive view of the adversary process as a game, and that requires us to ignore the extruded consequence: an aggrieved citizen unvindicated, a guilty man set loose, and a lawless constable substantially unpunished. Under such a concept it is the criminal who becomes, perversely, the instrument of justice. His freedom is somehow transmuted into the policeman's castigation. This singular paralogism, incredibly, is very widely accepted. Professor Dallin Oaks has already been quoted on the subject of our system's "limitless patience with irrationality." He went on to say that the release of two guilty men "would not be an excessive cost for an effective remedy against police misconduct, but it is a prohibitive price to pay for an illusory one."

It soon became, as I say, a corollary of *Miranda* that the jury may not consider any evidence to which the prosecution is led by the defendant if the interrogation violated *Miranda*. If—let us say—an apprehended murderer should blurt out the whereabouts of the murder weapon as sitting in a place the police would never have uncovered on their own, but it is later on successfully argued that the accused had not intelligently waived the advice of a lawyer who, when he is summoned, objects to his client's having been asked the question, the trial must proceed as though the whereabouts of the murder weapon were completely unknown. (The theatrical imposition on the prosecutor is itself interesting. Beyond that, we have another extension of the game-analogue: the benching of a member of the hockey team, so that the bad team plays on, understrength.) They call this the "fruit of the poisoned tree," the consumption of which is forbidden, even as it was prohibited to Eve to taste the fruit—of knowledge. Chief Justice Roger Traynor of California put it well (*People v. Cahan*) in 1955: "The rules of evidence are designed to enable courts to reach the truth and, in criminal cases, to secure a fair trial to those accused of crime. Evidence obtained by an illegal search and seizure is ordinarily just as true and reliable as evidence lawfully obtained. The court needs all reliable evidence material to the issue before it, the guilt or innocence of the accused, and how such evidence is

obtained is immaterial to that issue. It should not be
excluded unless strong considerations of public policy
demand it."

The course of the Fifth Amendment over the past
generation has not been reflected upon by students of
moderation. Judge Henry Friendly, lately of the Court of
Appeals, warns that the Court appears bent on taking
the Fifth to such lengths as might make every reporting
device unconstitutional. In 1965 (*Albertson v. Subversive
Activities Control Board*) the Court invalidated a provision
of the law which required members of the Communist
Party to register. Later (*Marchetti v. United States*), the
Court struck down the registration provisions of the
federal wagering tax and a part of the National Firearms
Act penalizing the illegal possession of unregistered
firearms. Judge Friendly warns of "the domino method of
Constitutional adjudication . . . wherein every explana-
tory statement in a previous opinion is made the basis for
extension to a wholly different situation. . . . High on the
vulnerable list," he warns, "are statutes, doubtless existing in almost every state, requiring the reporting of
automobile or other accidents and of compliance with
factory and building regulations and other safety and
sanitary standards."

C. Dickerman Williams illustrates the logical result of
the developing situation: "X was in New York City on
February 1, 1955. A number of crimes were committed in
New York on that day, but X participated in none of
them and X knows of no evidence that he did. In some
litigation X's presence in New York on February 1, 1955
becomes relevant. He is asked where he was on that day.
The witness invokes the Fifth . . . on the grounds that to
answer the question would constitute a link in a chain of
evidence exposing him to criminal prosecution."

The privilege against self-incrimination extends to all

pretrial proceedings. Moreover judges and prosecutors are nowadays forbidden to call to the attention of the jury that the accused has not taken the stand, nor may they inform the jury that the defendant refused to give evidence at pretrial proceedings. California tried. A provision of the state constitution, while confirming the privilege against self-incrimination, provided that "in any criminal case, whether the defendant testifies or not, his failure to explain or deny by his testimony any evidence or facts in the case against him may be commented upon by the court and by counsel, and may be considered by the court or the jury." But in 1965 the Supreme Court (*Griffin v. California*) held *that* unconstitutional, a decision we will in due course consider. Whereupon, Mr. Griffin, having been convicted of murder by the jury, was set free. It is only surprising that the Court has not got around to ordering that all written records of Griffin's original conviction should be vaporized.

Miranda and its constellation have done more than anything since the invention of human verbosity to delay, prolong, and complicate criminal trials. Nowadays there are frequently, in effect, two trials: the conventional trial and—before or alongside it—the trial within a trial, to test the exclusionary rule; to determine whether the statements of a witness, or the evidence he led to the discovery of, are admissible under *Miranda* et al. It being the principal purpose of this essay to stress the need for speedier justice for the sake of justice, I stress *this* effect of *Miranda*—the awful expenditure of castrate judicial energy devoted to the prophylactic enterprise of keeping defendant and jury apart.

What then, the Fifth Amendment apart, might be done? Here is a package of possible reforms, based on the assumption that the Court is not immovable.

Title II of the Crime Control and Safe Streets Act of 1968, in fact, attempts to repeal *Miranda*. The law has not yet been tested by the Supreme Court, but it is held unlikely by some shrewd Court-watchers that the Court will let it pass—on the grounds that *Miranda* is an extension of the Constitution and therefore beyond the reach of Congressional statute. This view is held even on the assumption that before very long a majority of the Court will have been appointed by Richard Nixon. There is the argument that the new majority, as strict constructionists, would probably not want to allow a constitutional clarification—even one they disagree with —to be negated by statute, thereby encouraging the notion that the easiest way to change the Constitution is to change the constitution of the Court (which, as a matter of fact, is exactly correct). But it is imprudent, in speaking of the Court, to reason or even to speculate schematically about it, as though it were a single political or philosophical intelligence. However, the Court, we need to remind ourselves, is composed of nine men who as often as not are furiously at loggerheads with one another. There is some reason to suppose that the Court would welcome aggressive, if rhetorically deferential, action by Congress.

Consider, for example, the last major opinion on search and seizure (*Coolidge v. New Hampshire,* 1971). I love *Coolidge*. It is one of my very favorites. . . . So the police, suspecting Coolidge of a brutal murder, go to see his wife. Outside the house sits a car answering the description of the murderer's car. The police open the door and take a look. They pull out evidence of Coolidge's guilt. Everyone concedes that if a magistrate had been there, he'd have issued a warrant to search the car. Coolidge was convicted. Citing as inadmissible the evidence taken from the car, the Court reversed. The plurality opinion of Justice Stewart referred to the constitutional provision on the subject as an "uncertain mandate." The Warren Court had overruled itself twenty-seven times in its own decisions on search and seizure. In *Coolidge*, a dissenting opinion by Justice White criticized the plurality opinion not merely as "unexplained," but as "inexplicable." Justice Stewart described Justice White's opinion, in turn, as "nonsense." Separate opinions by Justices Black and Harlan disagreed with the fundamental rationale of the plurality opinion, Justice Harlan noting that the law on search and seizure needed an "overhauling."

The new package of rules might be advanced as designed to restore the balance between the prosecution and the defense. It is a package that would take into account disadvantages to the defendant which are unnecessary and unfair.

—A defendant who is otherwise willing to take the witness stand and answer questions may nevertheless elect not to do so if he has a previous criminal record, because although the jury is instructed not to permit itself to be influenced by the fact of such a record when deciding the defendant's guilt or innocence, the prosecution may bring up the record for the purpose of impeaching the witness's credibility. The rule allowing disclosure of prior convictions on the issue of credibility should be revoked.

—The defendant is generally (there are differences among the states) brought to trial upon indictment by a grand jury. He is not privy to what was said before the grand jury, and he is not entitled to question the prosecution in advance of the trial, which would permit him to prepare his defense thoroughly. Sometimes preliminary hearings are scheduled at which the magistrate decides whether finally to commit the case to trial.

However, even then there isn't full disclosure by the prosecution. The prosecution can deal out only just enough of its cards to persuade the magistrate that there are prima facie grounds for going to trial, saving the trumps for the real jury. The grand jury should be eliminated (where constitutionally possible), as was done in England in 1933. At the hearing, the prosecution should be required to present all its evidence and pledge to furnish the accused with any supplementary evidence it comes up with before the trial. It is likelier that with full knowledge of the prosecution's case, the guilty defendant will plead guilty; while the innocent defendant, preparing an adequate defense, is all the more likely to win acquittal. Sixteen years ago Judge Jerome Frank wrote a book called *Not Guilty* in which he examined the cases of a number of defendants who, events proved, had been wrongly convicted. He concluded that pretrial discovery would have avoided every one of these miscarriages of justice. And he concluded that the defendant's constitutional rights had in each case been scrupulously observed.

—On the prosecutor's side, the accused would be advised upon being taken into custody of his right to remain silent and of his right to counsel, either retained or supplied at public expense. He would be reminded that any assertion of innocence could not be investigated without the help of the accused.

—Soon after the arrest, if possible within twenty-four hours, a magistrate would advise the accused, at a thorough examination, that the questions being put to him were being recorded on videotape so that at any subsequent trial the jurors could see and hear exactly what took place. This procedure would, incidentally, banish any possibility of surreptitious torture.

—At the trial, the witness could again speak or remain

silent, but any part of the viedotape could be shown to point out contradictions in his testimony.

The suggestion is that showing the jury the tape is qualitatively different from calling to its attention the witness's silence before the magistrate, and that therefore the Court might find a legitimate basis for distinction from the case of *Griffin v. California.* And *Miranda*, though not contradicted, would be modified by the questioning done before a magistrate with full exposure of the accused's statements, or silence. The Court itself, in *Miranda*, recognized that the rules laid down could be changed provided that the new rules were as effective in guarding the rights of the defendant. The package here proposed is faithful to the rules in apprising defendants of the right of silence and giving them an adequate opportunity to exercise it. But, though this approach should be attempted, in the end, the Fifth Amendment, as currently exercised, should be dropped.

I judge the effective repeal of the Fifth Amendment, as presently used, to be the single most important procedural reform designed to rescue the adversary process from discredit as a game engaged in by decadent professional enthusiasts whose vision of the purposes of justice has degenerated into a thoughtless ritual in behalf of the defendant class.

The Fifth Amendment used to constitute a procedural guarantee that confessions had been voluntarily given, and were therefore reliable guides to what actually had happened, and who was responsible. Gradually, under pressure of the civil liberties lobby, the courts found themselves stressing not so much whether the confession was voluntary, but whether the police had observed an increasingly formalistic ritual of interrogation.

The relevant clause of the Fifth Amendment to the

Constitution reads, "No person shall be . . . compelled in any criminal case to be a witness against himself." That is all. In France the simple privilege survives—no one can be required to testify against himself, in the sense of being punished if he declines to do so. But the prosecution can dwell as it likes, before the jury, on the defendant's silence. So should it be here.

"No one who reads the Fifth Amendment to the Constitution," writes Professor Sidney Hook (*Common Sense and the Fifth Amendment*), "without reference to the decisions of the U.S. Supreme Court could possibly understand the meaning and scope of its [self-incrimination] provision [as it has developed over the years]." As interpreted by the Supreme Court, the Fifth Amendment is not restricted to a "criminal" case; nor is it limited to use by defendants. "It covers *all* witnesses," as Mr. Hook points out. It can be invoked "not only in court proceedings but in any kind of legislative proceeding." In 1950 it was interpreted by the Supreme Court "as meaning, in effect, that a witness need not answer *any* question a truthful answer to which might furnish 'a link in the chain of evidence' required for prosecution (*Blair v. U.S.*)."

As a practical matter, a witness can nowadays get away with pleading the Fifth Amendment for any reason whatsoever, inasmuch as there are no settled mechanics by which to discover whether he is using the Fifth in order to protect himself (legal); in order to protect others (illegal); in order to spite the judge (illegal and contemptuous); or in order to incriminate someone else (illegal and dastardly). And, as we have noted, it is no longer permitted to draw to the jury's attention that the defendant has taken the Fifth. The privilege of the Fifth Amendment stops only where most privileges stop, at the gates of Internal Revenue. In 1927 (*United States v.*

Sullivan) the Court said that an individual who has acquired income by illicit means is not excused from making out an income tax return because he might thereby expose himself to a criminal prosecution by the United States. "He could [otherwise] draw a conjurer's circle around the whole matter," said Justice Holmes—who, on another occasion, said that he didn't mind paying taxes, that was what he "bought civilization with."

There are strong arguments for repealing the Fifth Amendment altogether, others for greatly restricting the availability of it, and still others for encouraging the inference of guilt on the part of those who invoke it. Montesquieu's stricture is in point: "[We] must not separate the Laws from the End for which they were made." The End of the Laws is to apprehend and punish the guilty. Does the Fifth Amendment further that end? And again Montesquieu: "We must not separate the Laws from the Circumstances in which they were made." Do the circumstances that led to the Fifth Amendment, i.e., the widespread use of torture, now prevail?

The phrase *"nemo tenetur seipsum prodere"*—no man shall be compelled to proceed against himself—developed in response to Star Chamber excesses. It meant, simply, that no one should be put on trial and compelled to answer questions unless he had first been properly accused, i.e., by a grand jury's agreeing that a prima facie case against him existed.

Those who speak of the Fifth Amendment as a natural right, i.e., as a right the deprivation of which amounts to nothing less than an attrition of the human condition, should be required to weigh empirically the meaning of natural rights. After all, any enumeration of natural rights requires attention to the historical context, the character of a people, that sort of thing. For instance, freedom of speech, though perhaps a natural right in any abstract catalogue, could not be held to be a significant right among illiterate peoples. The freedom of the press took on importance only after the invention of—the press. With the elimination of the Star Chamber, and the precautions technology makes available against torture, the Fifth Amendment's standing as an empirically important right is impossible to establish, whatever its metaphysical presumptions.

In fact, the argument of natural rights works against the Fifth Amendment. "The great and chief end of men uniting into commonwealths, and putting themselves under government," John Locke (among others) stressed, "is . . . the mutual preservation of their lives, liberties and estates." The government cannot do its best to assure that preservation in the absence of the power to compel witnesses to give evidence—even if that evidence is damaging to their own interests.

The Fifth Amendment is almost always referred to as a "privilege" as distinguished from a "right." It isn't often enough observed that the invocation of this privilege can have the effect of impairing a right. The Fifth Amendment is unjust to victims of crime, and to potential victims of the guilty who, escaping punishment, resume their criminal careers.

As recently as in 1968, Joseph Weintraub, the Chief Justice of New Jersey (*State v. McKnight*), arguing against extension of the privilege, put the distinctions in perspective. "The Constitution is not at all offended when a guilty man stubs his toe. On the contrary, it is decent to hope that he will. . . . Thus the Fifth Amendment does not say that a man shall not be permitted to incriminate himself, or that he shall not be persuaded to do so. It says no more than that a man shall not be 'compelled' to give evidence against himself."

In 1937, before the defense of the Fifth Amendment became fanatical—in part because it was understood as a means of objecting to McCarthyism—Justice Benjamin Cardozo made comments about the Fifth (*Palko v. Connecticut*) with which Justices Black, Stone, Hughes, and Brandeis associated themselves. They are startling. "Few would be so narrow or provincial"—here he was clearly wrong—"as to maintain that a fair and enlightened system of justice would be impossible without . . . immunity from compulsory self-incrimination. . . . This too might be lost, and justice still be done. Indeed, today as in the past there are students of our penal system who look upon the immunity as a mischief rather than a benefit, and who would limit its scope, or destroy it altogether. No doubt there would remain the need to give protection against torture, physical or mental. . . . Justice, however, would not perish if the accused were subject to a duty to respond to orderly inquiry."

Ernest Carmen stressed this point. "Let the most ardent advocate of constitutional privilege to the criminal point out a single case in all the annals of American jurisprudence where an innocent man has been, or could have been, convicted because compelled to answer questions about the crime of which he was accused."

Concretely, on the matter of what protections would survive the elimination of the disputed clause in the Fifth Amendment: The right against unreasonable search and seizure (Fourth Amendment); the due process clause (Fifth and Fourteenth); the compulsory process for obtaining witnesses (Sixth); the right to a speedy and public trial (Sixth); the right to trial by jury (Seventh); the protection against cruel and unusual punishment (Eighth); plus a series of Supreme Court decisions that relate to these amendments and elaborate the rights of the defendant. The argument that the Fifth Amendment is necessary in order to prevent the practice of the third degree is fanciful, because existing statutory laws make most third-degree practices illegal, and anyone who is arrested can refuse to reply to any question whatsoever pending the advice of counsel. Indeed, a defendant's confession can be ruled illegal without any reference at all to the Fifth Amendment if the circumstances suggest coercion.

At a less august level than doing away with the Fifth in the quest for speedier justice, one notes that our judicial system is staffed on the assumption that 90 percent of all cases will be disposed of without trial. Reduce that figure to 80 percent, and, by current practices, you would need twice as many judges, jurors, lawyers, clerks, stenotypists —the lot.

The imperatives of speedy justice serve not merely the abstract obligation of the state to the aggrieved party. They serve the goal of crime deterrence. The effectiveness of swift and sure (though not necessarily heavy) punishment is the only deterrent whose effectiveness is everywhere conceded. Edward Bennett Williams makes the point: "If punishment really is to work, it doesn't have to be severe, but it has to be swift. Now, in England, I spent a whole summer watching the British system work several years ago. If a man is convicted in Old Bailey today, via a jury of his English peers, three weeks later he's in the British Court of Criminal Appeals, and a decision comes down that very day." This statement, by perhaps the leading criminal lawyer in the United States, is professionally and personally interesting. Mr. Williams, as a philosopher, condemns the law's delays. As a practitioner, he must do the best he can to play out his clients' best interests, as the laws of the game permit; and his best is formidable. The wonder is not that so many months go by before Mr. Williams' clients come to trial, but that they ever come to trial.

There is urgent reason, then, to clear the decks.

—A good place to begin is by easing away from judicial concern over "victimless crimes." The term is, to be sure, glib, requiring for its authority that one lean heavily on the dictum of Mill that the state has no legitimate concern to protect anyone from himself. Yet that is a bit of High English rationality that does not itself, for instance, cope adequately with such a question as whether the father of three children is harming only himself by mainlining heroin. Still, a sensible society listens especially hard to the libertarian chorus when crime rises, and, as a matter of common sense if not of philosophical rectitude, it ceases to use its police, prosecutors, courts, and jails to track down pimps and prostitutes, gamblers and drunkards. In Atlanta, in 1968, there were forty thousand arrests for drunkenness. In St. Louis, a city of approximately the same size, there were five hundred and sixty arrests for drunkenness during the same year. If we make the modest assumption that people in St. Louis drink about as much, per capita, as people in Atlanta, we conclude that the police of St. Louis are instructed to let all but the most obstreperous drunkards alone, while in Atlanta the police are instructed to bring them in. There are no figures to suggest that arresting the drunkard is improving the quality of life in Atlanta over against the quality of life in St. Louis, but one must assume that the length of time required to arrest, book, jail, and fine forty thousand people takes several times forty thousand hours of time that might otherwise be spent in making life harder for those in Atlanta who rob, mug, rape, and murder.

—Chief Justice Warren Burger asked, in his State of the Judiciary speech in 1970, that a joint commitment be made by all parties to try criminal cases within sixty days after indictment, "and let us see what happens." (What happened is that no such commitment was made, so we do not know what would happen.) Lyndon Johnson's Presidential Commission on Law Enforcement and the Administration of Justice, recognizing that pretrial motions are a major source of delay, recommended that, barring exceptional circumstances, all such motions and other pretrial applications be filed within ten days of arraignment (which would follow the preliminary hearing by one to three days), that arguments on such motions be heard within one week, and that the judge decide them within three weeks of argument. That, by English standards, is a pretty leisurely timetable, but it is a vast improvement over current practice in the United States.

—Professor Delmar Karlen of New York University makes a point here not usually heard. It is that the American penchant for putting everything in writing is not only colossally expensive, but colossally time-consuming. Not infrequently a judge considers the same case three times before reaching his decision. First when he studies the briefs of counsel. Second when he hears oral argument. And finally when he prepares his opinion or reviews that of one of his colleagues. If the judge is normal, he has, between each stage, forgotten much of what he focused on earlier, and needs to review his thinking. Cases are not heard and decided one by one but in batches. A court may sit to hear arguments in twenty or more cases during a single week, then adjourn for four or five weeks while the judges prepare their opinions, and study the briefs for the batch of cases next scheduled for oral argument. In England the procedure is basically oral. Written briefs not only are not required, they are not permitted; and the judges usually render their decisions extemporaneously, and immediately upon the close of argument by counsel. In England, appellate delays of the type that occur in the United States are simply unknown. Nor is the quality of English justice demonstrably inferior to our own.

—Unnecessary paperwork is of course a great enemy of expeditious justice, and the courts wallow in it. One suspects that is why many judges, drawn by multiple literary, moral, and philosophical temptations, spend so much time Dutch-uncling about this and that, rather than focusing on the issues at stake. Many of them are clearly distracted from the question whether such error as occurred was harmless—insufficient to warrant a new trial. Opinions run to dozens of pages, in a style appropriate to law review articles, assuming any style is appropriate to law review articles. Much of the discussion is peripheral: dilations on police conduct, law reform, rules of conduct for police, prosecutors, trial judges, lesser divinities. *Cui bono?* The administration of justice, after all that accumulated advice, is worse than it was by any criterion.

—Judge David Peck, lately of New York's appellate court, has estimated that a jury trial takes three times as long as trials conducted by judges. Others guess it up to ten times as long. Yet there would appear to be no need for juries to try lesser misdemeanors, and already states vary in their requirements of juries, the Supreme Court having ruled (*Baldwin*, 1970) that the Sixth Amendment's guarantee of a jury trial in criminal proceedings need not apply in "petty offenses," carrying less than a six-month penalty. The Constitution requires juries only for "capital or otherwise infamous crimes." In England, magistrates do the trying of misdemeanors. And in England, in 1967, the requirement that juries reach unanimous verdicts was revoked. It is now demanded only that they reach a verdict of ten out of twelve. The Supreme Court has ruled that it is not a constitutional requirement that jury findings be unanimous. And surely juries are not needed to adjudicate disputes over the law? Why did Dan Ellsberg need a jury, when the fact of his having given over the classified documents to the New York *Times* was not disputed? Why did Sirhan need a jury to weigh the question of "diminished responsibility"?

We can see, by drawing back a little, accretions on judicial practice which reflect the extension of the game principle. If one team is free to take time out when the ball is on its own five-yard line—then the other team should be free to make substitutions during the time out: it has been going that way. It would not greatly matter, except that the results are, really, quite appalling, and the point is being lost. And since the United States, more than any other civilized country, is given to the uproarious practice of crime, America needs to be more flexible than any other country in searching out nonbarbarous ways of doing something about it. "Our procedure has always been haunted by the ghost of the innocent man convicted," Judge Learned Hand said. "It is an unreal dream. What we need to fear is the archaic formalism and the watery sentiments that obstruct, delay, and defeat the prosecution of crime." And Justice White, dissenting on *Miranda*, let out his exasperation whole: "The most basic function of any government is to provide for the security of the individual and of his property. These ends of society are served by the criminal laws which for the most part are aimed at the prevention of crime. Without the reasonably effective performance of the task of preventing private violence and retaliation, it is idle to talk about human dignity and civilized values."

An Afterword

WE are all haunted by the thought that self-government will prove too great a burden; that, in the phrase of Michael Oakeshott, we are doomed to be individuals manqués. We know, about self-government, what the no-nonsense historical actuaries can tell us, namely that a nation's experience with it is likely to be short-lived, very short-lived. One can always point to an England or a Switzerland, but so can the actuary point to the man in Central Asia who is 125 years old: the incidence of such people does not greatly affect the table of probabilities—the macro-statistics overwhelm us. Self-rule flowered as an idea in the nineteenth century after a very long sleep of almost two thousand years, and by the early part of the twentieth century it had become ideologized, and wars were fought in its name. J. S. Mill would talk about democracy as a condition as predictable as biological maturity, as an instinct as imperative and as glamorous as sex. Woodrow Wilson's war to make the world safe for democracy brought a rebuke, in postwar Germany and Russia, at once grotesque and pixieish, and by the time "democracy" was listed, one war later, in the United Nations Declaration of Human Rights as primus inter

pares, the word had become sheer incantation, as in the
"Democratic Republic of Germany." So much virtue
having been invested in the word, the easiest road for
totalitarian or despotic or one-party states was not to
reject the word, but to pervert its meaning.

Soon after the decolonization of Africa it became clear
that the new nations would march, after a brief and
usually bloody interlude, from rule by a foreign parliament to rule by an indigenous dictator. For a short season
there was indignation over this, but the chorus calmed
down quickly, and one hears nothing more about it, nor
is it anywhere anticipated that the countries in question
will break loose from despotic forms after a few years'
experience. Across the South Atlantic, in another conti-
nent that broke away from colonialism, there was
dwindling democracy a century after liberation. It sometimes seems as though the world concerts ghoulishly to
rebuke the century of democratic optimism by ushering
in a century preordained yearly to offer up one parliament, in return for one strong man.

By Latin American standards the United States has
done pretty well. But there is a developing national
intuition that insofar as one is spared one-party or
one-man rule, one must oblige other authority in other
forms. Conventionally there is the strong parliament or
the strong executive or the strong judiciary. At another
level there is the authority of the dominating, domi-
neering, myths. "Economic democracy" is an example of
one; "equality" is another, related example; "the melting
pot" has been strong: secular humanism the sunless sky
blanketing them all. These would appear to have served
the national ethos in giving us a sense of direction and,
above all, that sense of security that people appear to feel
only when they submit to adamantine political leader-
ship: a de Gaulle, replacing a Fourth Republic with a

Fifth Republic which, substantially, was—himself, in the royal French tradition. The myths have served as national tropisms, attracting supporters, votaries even, who accept the myths as pregnant historically with humanitarian idealism, as ethically refined and ennobling, and, when they call for self-discipline, as properly chastening. There is a very good reason for not scrutinizing every myth that proves socially useful. But when those myths grow in imposture, sinking deep and proliferating roots, they strain republican self-esteem. We have cultivated several great superstitions in the past generation, and we live with them precariously as substitutes for the stabler ideals of reason, faith, charity—and self-rule. We are encouraged to believe that the federal government breeds money, that rich people can support nonrich people, that oversecularized, racially integrated education can breed a harmonious and civilized citizenry, and that we move towards justice by forever elaborating the rights and privileges of the accused. These procedural superstitions, sprinkled over our laws and our rhetoric, are the holy water of liberal ideology.

To shake loose! It is the politicians who have the formal powers: to amend constitutions, to pass the laws, to revise the ordinances. The politicians respond, when they do at all, not so much to public clamor, which is usually ephemeral; hardly ever to public velleities, which are safely ignored; occasionally to argument which is at once cogent and, above all, timely. The American experience with self-rule is largely negative: the people are fairly good at going to the polls and saying No to the incumbent, as to the challenger; and this was, is, and forever will be the principal housekeeping use of democracy. But sometimes there is generated what the kids give a bad name to by attaching it recently to preposterous goals—the nonnegotiable demand. We can see that some (not all) of the provisions of the civil rights bills of the sixties were in that category. So much time is spent on vapid exhortation in a democracy, one's ear tends to discount it. But every day laws *are* passed, and every now and then the people experience the delights of reasoned self-rule, and then true reforms are made.